Frontiers in Chinese Linguistics

Volume 10

Frontiers in Chinese Linguistics (FiCL) is a book series jointly published by Springer-Nature and Peking University Press. FiCL aims to publish original and innovative research outcome in the fast expanding and developing discipline of Chinese language sciences. FiCL welcomes submissions of proposals of the following types of books on issues related to Chinese language and linguistics: selection of post-conference papers from leading edge prestigious conferences and workshops; monograph on research with potential to open new frontiers; and outstanding dissertations dealing with new issues and new methodologies. FiCL volumes will be published by Springer with worldwide distribution and by Peking University Press in China. FiCL is the sister series of 语言学前沿, a prestigious book series published in Chinese by Peking University Press introducing new theories and new ideas in Chinese linguistics.

More information about this series at http://www.springer.com/series/15591

Qingqing Zhao

Embodied Conceptualization or Neural Realization

A Corpus-Driven Study of Mandarin Synaesthetic Adjectives

北京大学出版社
PEKING UNIVERSITY PRESS

Springer

Qingqing Zhao
Institute of Linguistics
Chinese Academy of Social Sciences
Beijing, China

ISSN 2522-5308 ISSN 2522-5316 (electronic)
Frontiers in Chinese Linguistics
ISBN 978-981-32-9314-4 ISBN 978-981-32-9315-1 (eBook)
https://doi.org/10.1007/978-981-32-9315-1

Jointly published with Peking University Press
The print edition is not for sale in China Mainland. Customers from China Mainland please order the print book from: Peking University Press.

This Springer imprint is published by the registered company Springer Nature Singapore Pte Ltd.
The registered company address is: 152 Beach Road, #21-01/04 Gateway East, Singapore 189721, Singapore

Preface

Qualia in psychology and philosophy represents the experiential knowledge of human beings. In linguistics, it is best known in the context of the theory of Generative Lexicon. It goes without saying that experiential knowledge is highly dependent on sensory input. Hence, the study of the sensory lexicon and the linguistic manipulation of sensory words can shed light on how experiential knowledge is conceptualized and lexicalized. Given the above background, it is perhaps not surprising that Dr. Zhao Qingqing built upon her earlier training in Generative Lexicon theory to focus her Ph.D. study on linguistics synaesthesia, one of the most direct windows to examining how sensory concepts interact, as well as how language may constrain the sensory lexicon.

For those readers who do not yet have a good idea of what synaesthesia means, please go ahead and read this book to learn about this exciting subject. As a reviewer for the Thesis of the Year in Chinese Linguistics notes, "[This] book … is well organized and is written with great clarity and coherence…." For those of you who are working on metaphors and synaesthesia, you will find many new topics and research questions based on a comprehensive set of data and accounts that challenge conventional wisdom. For those who come from the background of neuro-cognitive studies of synaesthesia, you will find exciting links and comparisons to similar findings and contrasting approaches in your field. For those who are interested in language and culture, you will find thc culture- and language-dependent mapping directionalities of synaesthesia fascinating.

Dr. Zhao is a dedicated and conscientious scholar who is careful and meticulous with her data, as well as thorough and open-minded in exploring related literature and alternative accounts in different disciplines. She has been a pleasure to collaborate with as a student and as a colleague. Her results presented in this book have shed light on some of the most intricate parts of the mosaic of senses as realized in linguistic synesthesia. I have no doubt that her own future work and work based on insights from this book will help us to make better sense of the sensory lexicon in the future.

June 2019

Chu-Ren Huang
Chair Professor, Department of Chinese and Bilingual Studies, The Hong Kong Polytechnic University
Hong Kong

Acknowledgements

This book is mainly based on my Ph.D. thesis at The Hong Kong Polytechnic University. Thus, it would not have been possible without the valuable support I received from many people during my Ph.D. studies.

I would first like to give my sincerest gratitude to my brilliant, supportive, and inspiring supervisor, Prof. Huang Chu-Ren. I am deeply grateful that he is always available to provide constructive comments on my research, always generous in sharing his own inspiring ideas, and always considerate in creating stimulating networks for young scholars.

My deep gratitude also goes to my co-supervisor, Dr. Lee Yat-mei Sophia, several research fellows in PolyU, and two external thesis examiners. Dr. Lee always offers insightful feedback on my drafts promptly and has given generous financial support to my research. Dr. Yao Yao from the Department of Chinese and Bilingual Studies, Prof. Ahrens Kathleen and Dr. Tay Dennis, both from the Department of English, have also provided valuable comments on my project. Dr. Kwong Oi Yee from the Chinese University of Hong Kong and Dr. Wang Xian Vincent from the University of Macau have given detailed suggestions to improve my thesis.

My family has offered consistent support during my pursuit of an academic career. I am greatly indebted to my father, Zhao Zhiyou, my mother, Huang Enju, my husband, Zhang Bing, and my new-born son, Zhang Luming for their full support and unconditional love.

Contents

Abbreviations

ASP	Aspect
AUX	Auxiliary
CL	Classifier
CMT	Conceptual Metaphor Theory
GEN	Genitive
LSIP	Linguistic synaesthesia identification procedure
MED	Middle English Dictionary
MIP	Metaphor identification procedure
MIPVU	Metaphor identification procedure VU University Amsterdam
NEG	Negation
NOM	Nominalization
OED	Oxford English Dictionary
PAR	Particle
PL	Plural

Chapter 1
Introduction to Synaesthesia

Synaesthesia, with an alternative spelling as *synesthesia*, has the etymological roots *syn* 'together' and *aisthesia* 'perception' in Greek (Popova 2005; Ronga et al. 2012). It describes a situation where perceptions in different sensory modalities are associated in both perceptual experiences and linguistic expressions (Ullmann 1957; Williams 1976; Cytowic 1993; Shen and Eisenman 2008).[1]

The association of sensory modalities in perceptual experiences, named "neurological synaesthesia" alternatively, is an uncommon phenomenon in which a capacity to experience sensations in one modality is manifested when a different modality is stimulated, or a percept in one sub-modality is elicited by stimulus belonging to another sub-modality. Examples include tasting shapes, perceiving colors from black-printed graphemes, and so on (see Cytowic 1993, 2002 [1989]; Banissy et al. 2015). Neuroscientists, such as Ramachandran and Hubbard (2001) and Hubbard and Ramachandran (2005), have suggested that synaesthesia in perceptual experiences is a neural disorder caused by defective pruning of connections between brain regions. However, more recent studies, such as Ward et al. (2006), Marks and Mulvenna (2013), and Banissy et al. (2014), have considered neurological synaesthesia a special cognitive condition. These studies have assumed that neurological synaesthesia recruits cross-modal mechanisms perceptually and cognitively common to all human beings rather than special neural pathways absent for most people.

Synaesthesia in linguistic expressions, also termed as "linguistic synaesthesia" or "synaesthetic metaphor" in the literature, involves the description of perceptions in one sensory modality in terms of lexical items from other modalities (e.g., Yu 2003;

[1]It is interesting that the preference for the spellings of synaesthesia varies across regions and disciplines. For instance, the spelling with *a* (i.e., *synaesthesia*) is used frequently by European scholars, such as Ullmann (1957), while the spelling without *a* (i.e., *synesthesia*) is preferred by American researchers, such as Marks et al. (1987). Besides, the former spelling is generally chosen by linguists (e.g., Williams 1976), whereas the latter by neuroscientists (e.g., Ramachandran and Hubbard 2001). This book focusing on linguistic realizations of sensory associations will use the with-*a* spelling that is orthographically closer to the etymological origin of the term hereinafter.

Q. Zhao, *Embodied Conceptualization or Neural Realization*,
Frontiers in Chinese Linguistics 10, https://doi.org/10.1007/978-981-32-9315-1_1

Ronga et al. 2012; Strik Lievers 2017). Typological investigations conducted by Ullmann (1966 [1963]) and Viberg (1983) have found that this kind of language usage appears cross-linguistically. For instance, the English gustatory adjective *sweet* can be used to describe an auditory perception, as in the phrase *sweet voice*; and the Mandarin tactile adjective 冷 *leng3* 'cold' can modify a visual perception, as in the expression 冷色 *leng3 se4* 'cold color'.[2]

Extensive studies have been conducted on neurological synaesthesia to further out understanding of human perception and cognition (see Cytowic 2002 [1989]; Simner and Hubbard 2013; Banissy et al. 2015). By contrast, less attention has been given to linguistic synaesthesia, especially the widespread synaesthetic usages in non-poetic languages (Strik Lievers 2015; Zhao et al. 2018b). In addition, Rakova (2003) and Zhao et al. (2019) have demonstrated that linguistic synaesthesia would pose challenges to linguistic theories including Conceptual Metaphor Theory (CMT) and the theory of embodiment (see Lakoff and Johnson 1980, 1999), as concepts are mapped from one concrete sensory domain to another concrete sensory domain in linguistic synaesthesia, rather than from the concrete to the abstract as in canonical metaphors. Furthermore, the significant research value of linguistic synaesthesia in the examination of neurological synaesthesia and of the interaction between neuro-cognitive activities and linguistic conceptualizations has been confirmed by various studies, such as Cacciari (2008), Marks and Mulvenna (2013), Caballero and Paradis (2015), and so forth. Therefore, this book will focus on linguistic synaesthesia. More specifically, I will examine the transfer patterns and underlying mechanisms of linguistic synaesthesia in a hitherto less-studied language, Mandarin Chinese, and the nature of linguistic synaesthesia will be clarified based on the tendencies of Mandarin synaesthesia. Last but not least, the theoretical implications of linguistic synaesthesia will be shown, including refinement of CMT and the embodiment theory.

This chapter presents a review of the literature on linguistic synaesthesia in general and linguistic synaesthesia of Chinese in particular. A brief overview of this book will also be given at the end of the chapter.

1.1 Linguistic Synaesthesia

Previous research focuses on three main questions concerning linguistic synaesthesia: (1) what transfer tendencies does linguistic synaesthesia show; (2) what are the underlying mechanisms for synaesthetic mappings; and (3) is the nature of linguistic synaesthesia neurological (Ronga et al. 2012), metaphorical (Strik Lievers 2017), or literal (Winter 2019b).

[2]In order to avoid the controversial issue of whether synaesthesia in linguistic expressions is a metaphor or not (see Strik Lievers 2017; Winter 2019a), I will use the more neutral term "linguistic synaesthesia" throughout the book. Nevertheless, I will return to the dispute in Chap. 7.

1.1.1 Transfer Patterns

Existing studies on linguistic synaesthesia are most often based on Indo-European languages and focus on the transfer directions of lexical items between sensory modalities. These studies have all demonstrated that linguistic synaesthesia follows directionality tendencies (Ullmann 1957; Williams 1976; among others). Such tendencies are described in two different transfer models in the literature.

The first model originated from research on linguistic synaesthesia in poetic languages by Ullmann (1945, 1957, 1966 [1963]). Based on around 2000 synaesthetic examples collected from English, French, and Hungarian poems from the nineteenth century, Ullmann (1957) found that over 80% of the synaesthetic expressions conformed to the directional pattern described by the model in Fig. 1.1.

Shen (1997) confirmed this linear model for Hebrew poetry. In addition, Shen (1997), Shen and Cohen (1998), Shen and Eisenman (2008), and Shen and Gadir (2009) demonstrated the validity of the model with various experimental studies on linguistic synaesthesia in non-poetic Hebrew and English, which involved tasks such as interpretation generation, recall, naturalness judgements, and so forth. For example, they showed that synaesthetic expressions that conform to the directional tendency (e.g., *stinking paleness*) are easier to recall and are judged as more natural than expressions that violate the tendency (e.g., *pale stink*). Shen and Gil (2008) conducted both corpus-based and experimental studies on linguistic synaesthesia in Indonesian, showing that the directional tendency described in Fig. 1.1 also holds. However, all these studies on linguistic synaesthesia in non-Indo-European languages by Shen's team are based on a small data sample, in terms of both the corpus data for generalizing directional tendencies and the testing stimuli utilized in the cognitive experiments. For instance, Shen (1997) utilized 130 synaesthetic instances of poetic Hebrew and Shen and Gil (2008) employed 125 synaesthetic examples of non-poetic Indonesian to verify the transfer patterns of linguistic synaesthesia in each language. With respect to the experimental study by Shen and Gadir (2009), there are only two testing stimuli for each combination between any two of five senses.

Strik Lievers (2015) employed a larger data sample extracted automatically from the Wacky corpora (Baroni et al. 2009) through a computational approach to test the linear transfer model for linguistic synaesthesia in non-poetic English and Italian. The study verified the model in Fig. 1.1 for both English and Italian synaesthesia. Furthermore, Strik Lievers (2015: 69) claimed that the directional tendencies of linguistic synaesthesia should be interpreted as "frequency" rather than as absolute constraints. The claim entails that linguistic synaesthesia shows directional preferences, where synaesthetic mappings in one direction occur more frequently than those in the reverse direction, rather than stating that the mappings in the reverse direction cannot be found in real languages. However, Winter (2016a)

Touch → Taste → Smell → Hearing → Vision

Fig. 1.1 A linear model for linguistic synaesthesia

pointed out a flaw in Strik Lievers' (2015) corpus-based study with respect to methodology. That is, Strik Lievers (2015) did not take into consideration the distinction between types and tokens of synaesthetic transfers, both of which should be considered to determine the mapping directionality for linguistic synaesthesia (Winter 2016a).

Williams (1976) proposed a second linguistics synaesthesia transfer model, as shown in Fig. 1.2. By referring to the citation dates in the OED (Oxford English Dictionary) and MED (Middle English Dictionary), Williams generalized the model through focusing on adjectives used for more than one sensory domain in the history of English. Williams assumed that English sensory adjectives would follow this model when they changed their meanings among sensory modalities, and that if synaesthetic transfers violated the pattern, the resultant sensory meanings would become obsolete in the language. For instance, the study illustrated that the tactile meaning of the adjective *eager* was not retained in Standard English, although the adjective had a tactile meaning as the result of a transfer from taste to touch in the history of English (see Williams 1976: 476). Furthermore, Williams suggested that the hierarchy described in Fig. 1.2 should be applicable to any language, given the universality of the biological nature of human sensory modalities.

Lehrer's (1978) synchronic study on English sensory adjectives corroborated this model, but challenged the exclusive reliance on citations in dictionaries by Williams (1976), in consideration of the lack of written materials for earlier periods of English. She added that some unpredicted transfers by the model in Fig. 1.2 could still be used in English, such as the dimension item *fat* (belonging to vision) employed for taste (Lehrer 1978: 120).

The two transfer models assign an identical directional rank to touch, taste, and smell, as seen in Figs. 1.1 and 1.2. The main difference between the two models is the relationship between vision and hearing: While hearing precedes vision in Fig. 1.1, both directions between hearing and vision are possible in Fig. 1.2. The discrepancy is not, strictly speaking, contradictory, as Williams' (1976) model in Fig. 1.2 classified vision into two different sub-domains: dimension and color (Zhao et al. 2018b). Since both are models of directional tendencies that do not claim to be strict rules, the same set of data could be consistent in both models. In addition, Winter (2016a: 144) has observed that Williams' (1976) hierarchy of English synaesthesia is compatible with but stronger than Ullmann's (1957) linear model (cf. Fig. 1.1), as the former makes "more falsifiable" predictions and constraints for linguistic synaesthesia. In sum, studies on linguistic synaesthesia in

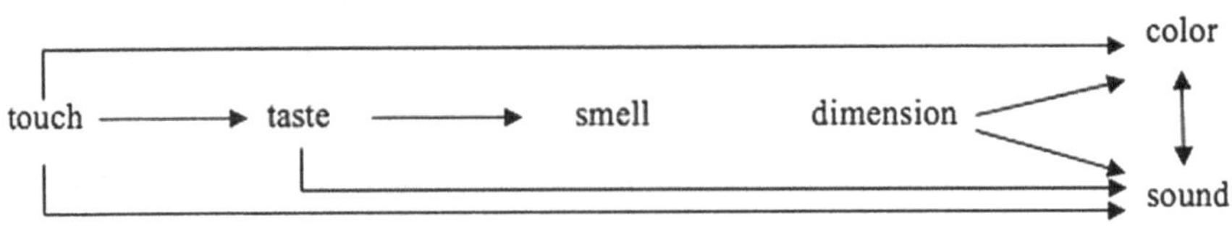

Fig. 1.2 A transfer hierarchy for linguistic synaesthesia (Williams 1976: 463)

Indo-European languages such as English and Italian, and non-Indo-European languages including Hebrew and Indonesian, have confirmed that different languages can share tendencies of directionality in synaesthetic transfers.

1.1.2 Underlying Mechanisms

There is a debate on the mechanisms underlying linguistic synaesthesia. One theoretical model was proposed in the framework of Cognitive Linguistics, which generally treats linguistic synaesthesia as a specific type of metaphor (Geeraerts 2010). This explanatory model claims that linguistic synaesthesia, similar to other types of metaphor, is also grounded in how our bodies experience the world, i.e., the perceived similarity of intensity and subjective evaluation (Shen 1997; Yu 2003; Popova 2005; among others). In this model, linguistic synaesthesia would follow the tendency of mapping from more embodied domains to less embodied ones, like other types of metaphor (see Lakoff and Johnson 1980; Johnson 1987).

In addition, as the source domain and the target domain of linguistic synaesthesia are both bodily and concrete sensory modalities, Shen (1997) argued that additional features should be introduced to differentiate the degrees of embodiment of different sensory perceptions. The study pointed out that touch and taste necessarily involve physical contact between sensory organs and perceived objects, while the other three modalities (i.e., vision, hearing, and smell) do not require such physical contact. Therefore, touch and taste are claimed to be more embodied than vision, hearing, and smell in Shen's work.

Shen (1997) also suggested that tactile perceptions, unlike other senses, do not require a specialized sensory organ, but instead have receptors all over the body. Hence, he proposed a rank of embodiment for five sensory modalities: touch is the most embodied sense, and taste follows, while vision, hearing, and smell are less embodied. Based on the ranking of the embodiment of five senses, Shen has contended that the directions of linguistic synaesthesia described in Fig. 1.1 (cf. pp. 5) are constrained by such embodiment mechanisms, i.e., mapping from the more embodied to the less embodied.

Similarly, Popova (2005: 416) suggested that embodiment is realized "at its strongest in touch," since scalarity and subjective evaluations of sensory stimuli dominate the perceptual experiences of touch (including taste), but not those of vision and hearing. Therefore, she assumed that the conceptualization of perceptual properties in vision and hearing in terms of concepts from touch and taste, illustrated the move from the more embodied to the less embodied.

The embodiment account for linguistic synaesthesia, however, has been criticized for its disregard of neural associations in the brain and of earlier occurrences of linguistic synaesthesia in the speech of young children compared to other types of metaphor. On the contrary, when we take the neural associations and the earlier occurrences into consideration, they might indicate that biological factors are at work (see Gardner 1974; Keil 1986; Marks et al. 1987; Seitz 1997, 2005). For instance, Ramachandran and Hubbard (2001: 18) have proposed that linguistic synaesthesia is the same as neurological synaesthesia, as both are shaped by "anatomical constraints" that permit "certain types of cross-activation, but not others." Seitz (2005: 90) pointed out that linguistic synaesthesia is an "inborn metaphorical association" that is "pre-wired" in brains.

Linguistic studies, such as Williams (1976) and Rakova (2003), also followed the biological association account for linguistic synaesthesia. For example, Rakova (2003) has suggested that the tactile meaning and the gustatory meaning of the English adjective *hot* are associated because of the same neural pain-detecting mechanism (i.e., VR1, Caterina et al. 1997), rather than through metaphorical mappings. In addition, Rakova (2003: 64) assumed that neurological synaesthesia is a "strong synaesthesia" and linguistic synaesthesia is a "weak synaesthesia," both of which are analogous with respect to the innate neural associations between senses.

The biological association account of linguistic synaesthesia has also been challenged. For instance, Day (1996) compared types of neurological synaesthesia documented in Cytowic (2002 [1989]) with linguistic synaesthesia collected from English and German novels. The research found that the two kinds of synaesthetic phenomena did not share the same patterns. For instance, colored sounds (i.e., the association between vision and hearing) were found to be the most common for neurological synaesthesia, while tactile sounds (i.e., the association between touch and hearing) were the most frequent for linguistic synaesthesia (Day 1996). Another criticism of the biological association account for linguistic synaesthesia is that the theory does not provide any explicit explanation for the directional tendency of linguistic synaesthesia (Popova 2005).

Zhao et al. (2018b) tested the two rival theoretical models of mechanisms underlying linguistic synaesthesia, based on their different predictions of synaesthetic tendencies in languages. The study attempted to determine whether the directionality of mappings from the more embodied to the less embodied for linguistic synaesthesia predicted by the embodiment account, or the cross-linguistic universality of transfer patterns suggested by the biological association account, can be supported by real linguistic data. Based on plentiful data from the Sinica corpus (Chen et al. 1996), the study found that distributions and tendencies of synaesthetic uses of gustatory adjectives in both Mandarin and English could not be explained or predicted by either single theory. Rather, linguistic synaesthesia can be accounted for by the combination of the two theories (Zhao et al. 2018b).

1.1.3 The Nature of Linguistic Synaesthesia

Linguistic synaesthesia, according to various studies, is a specific type of metaphor, and this view has become the "default" in the literature (Strik Lievers 2017: 87). For instance, Osgood et al. (1978 [1957]) and Geeraerts (2010) suggested that linguistic synaesthesia shared a similar nature with other types of metaphor in terms of describing one concept through another concept based on similar features. Apart from the rhetorical framework for metaphors, the CMT-based framework (Lakoff and Johnson 1980, 1999) has also recognized the metaphorical nature of linguistic synaesthesia, which manifests itself as mappings of concepts from more embodied domains to less embodied ones (e.g., Shen 1997; Yu 2003; Popova 2005). Strik Lievers (2017) also argued for linguistic synaesthesia as a particular type of metaphor, as there are conceptual conflicts between sensory concepts from the different modalities involved. However, as pointed out by Rakova (2003) and Peng and Bai (2008), linguistic synaesthesia is not the same as canonical metaphors that generally map from bodily domains to non-bodily domains (Steen 1999; Gibbs 2011).

Following CMT, metaphor is not only a matter of words, but also a conceptual mechanism structuring human thoughts and actions (Lakoff and Johnson 1980; Johnson 1987). Gibbs (2011) suggested that systematic metaphorical expressions using the concrete to describe the more abstract in different languages, such as LOVE IS A JOURNEY and ARGUMENT IS WAR, are crucial supporting evidence for metaphors not only in languages but also in conceptual systems. Nevertheless, linguistic synaesthesia has source domains and target domains that are both embodied and concrete sensory modalities. Thus, linguistic synaesthesia is different from canonical metaphors whose source domains exhibit an evident contrast with target domains concerning embodiment and concreteness.

Linguistic synaesthesia differs from canonical metaphors with respect to directional tendencies as well. Strik Lievers' (2015) corpus-based study has attested that linguistic synaesthesia does not follow absolute mapping directionality from the more embodied to the less embodied, as transfers violating this directional tendency can also be found in the language. For example, although transfers from touch to hearing occupy 23.2% of all English synaesthetic examples collected by Strik Lievers, there are still 0.2% of the total examples found to exhibit the transfer direction from hearing to touch (2015: 80). This pattern, however, has not been reported for typical metaphorical expressions mapping from the concrete to the abstract (see Lakoff and Johnson 1980; Sweetser 1990; Lakoff and Johnson 1999; among others).

Theoretical explanations for linguistic synaesthesia and metaphors are also not identical. For instance, Rakova (2003: 43) has assumed that linguistic synaesthesia could not be explained by theories of metaphor, since both source and target domains of linguistic synaesthesia are bodily and concrete perceptions without evident contrasts on "experiential primacy" and "conceptual primacy". Based on the corpus distribution of synaesthetic data, Zhao et al. (2018b) and Zhao and Huang (2018), have found that tendencies of linguistic synaesthesia cannot be accounted for or predicted completely by the embodiment mechanism which has been widely recognized to underlie typical metaphors conceptualizing non-bodily experiences in terms of bodily experiences (Lakoff and Johnson 1980; Sweetser 1990; Gibbs 2011).

Differences between linguistic synaesthesia and canonical metaphors can also be observed concerning research methodologies adopted. Studies on metaphorical expressions mainly begin with concepts expressed by lexical items (Steen 1999), based on which conceptual domains and mapping directions are determined subsequently (e.g., Clausner and Croft 1999; Paradis 2001; Grady 2005; Lien 2005; Ou 2014; among many others). Take the expression *my mind just isn't operating today*, for example (see Lakoff and Johnson 1980: 27). The contextual meaning of *operating* expresses a concept related to the mind. However, the lexical item *operating* has a literal meaning concerned with machines. Thus, *operating* can then be analyzed to illustrate the mapping from the conceptual domain of MACHINE to the conceptual domain of MIND in the example. Research on linguistic synaesthesia generally begins with the determination of sensory domains. Transfers of sensory items involving more than one sensory domain are then established (e.g., Ullmann 1957; Williams 1976; Shen 1997; Strik Lievers 2015; among many others). For instance, Williams (1976: 476) first distinguished six sensory domains, then determined the English adjective *sweet* had the original sensory domain of taste. As the adjective can have an auditory use in contemporary English, such as *sweet voice*, the study generalized the transfer direction from the sensory domain of taste to the sensory domain of hearing. Thus, unlike studies on metaphors that generally rely on a concept-based approach, studies on linguistic synaesthesia mainly employ a domain-based approach. It is intriguing that some canonical metaphor research, such as Ahrens (2002) and Chung et al. (2013), has also adopted the domain-based, rather than the concept-based, approach to examine metaphors, i.e., to investigate the interaction between established ontological knowledge and conceptual mappings in metaphors.

In short, linguistic synaesthesia manifesting itself as a mapping from one bodily experience to another bodily experience exhibits distinct characteristics from canonical metaphors. These distinct characteristics include: (1) the contrast of embodiment between source domains and target domains; (2) directional tendencies of mappings; (3) theoretical explanations; and (4) research methods adopted.

Apart from the differences between linguistic synaesthesia and canonical metaphors, the metaphorical claim about linguistic synaesthesia has been challenged by the growing body of research on neurological synaesthesia. For instance, Ramachandran and Hubbard (2001) and Ronga et al. (2012) hypothesized a neurological basis for linguistic synaesthesia, based on the "common origins and mechanisms" between neurological synaesthesia and linguistic synaesthesia. Ronga et al. (2012) employed a corpus-based approach to show that linguistic synaesthesia has parallels with neurological synaesthesia concerning the patterns of sensory associations. Asona and Yokosawa (2012) and Hung et al. (2014) found that similar patterns could be observed in neurological synaesthesia among people speaking different languages from different cultures. This finding could provide a support for the similarity between linguistic synaesthesia and neurological synaesthesia, as Willams (1976) suggested that transfer patterns of linguistic synaesthesia are cross-linguistically universal.

Winter (2019a, b) claimed that linguistic synaesthesia is neither metaphorical nor neurological in nature, but instead it is literal, as sensory words have "highly multisensory or supramodal meanings" in language (Winter, 2019a: 107). Take the English adjective *sweet*, for example. *Sweet fragrance* was considered the literal usage of *sweet*, as the adjective is supramodal involving both taste and smell (Winter 2019b: 125). The assumption is similar to Rakova's (2003) view, who suggests no distinctions between literal and metaphorical meanings of sensory adjectives with no perceptual and conceptual priorities on any sensory modality. As pointed out by Popova (2005), this literal claim on the nature of linguistic synaesthesia would be inconsistent with directional patterns of transfers in linguistic synaesthesia.

Therefore, the nature of linguistic synaesthesia has not been decided. It is still arguable whether linguistic synaesthesia can be properly analyzed as a specific type of metaphor, given the differences between linguistic synaesthesia and canonical metaphors and alternative assumptions on the nature of linguistic synaesthesia.

1.2 Linguistic Synaesthesia in Chinese

Linguistic synaesthesia in Chinese has not received as much attention as in Indo-European languages (Zhao et al. 2018b). Most earlier studies on Chinese synaesthesia tend to focus either on specific Chinese counterparts of English synaesthetic uses (e.g., Li 1996; Wang 2002; Wang and Xu 2002; Yang and Zhang 2007; Peng and Bai 2008; Wang 2008), or on synaesthetic usages in poetic Chinese (e.g., Qian 1985; Yu 2003). One exception is Lien's (1994) study on linguistic synaesthesia in one Chinese dialect Southern Min. The study proposed a unidirectional transfer hierarchy for synaesthetic words in Southern Min, where dimension is generally the lowest sense acting as the source domain for synaesthetic transfers, while smell is normally the highest modality as the target domain of linguistic synaesthesia. Therefore, Lien's (1994) model is different from the transfer models generalized for linguistic synaesthesia based on Indo-European languages, where touch is the lowest sensory modality as the productive source domain (cf. Sect. 1.1.1).

More recent research on Chinese synaesthesia has begun to examine language-specific characteristics of linguistic synaesthesia in Chinese, such as Xiong and Huang (2015), Zhao and Huang (2015), Zhao et al. (2015, 2018b, 2019), and Zhao and Huang (2018). These studies have shown that Chinese synaesthesia does exhibit different tendencies when compared with English synaesthesia. For instance, Xiong and Huang (2015) found that the gustatory adjective 苦 *ku3* 'bitter' in Mandarin Chinese could be used for the olfactory domain, while the gustatory adjective *bitter* in English did not show the transfer. Similarly, Zhao and Huang (2015) attested that the synaesthetic tendencies of Mandarin tactile, gustatory, and olfactory adjectives are not consistent with the hierarchy generalized by Williams (1976) for English sensory adjectives. Zhao et al. (2018b) employed a corpus-based approach to examine linguistic synaesthesia in Mandarin and English gustatory adjectives. The study confirmed that Mandarin and English did not share the same synaesthetic tendencies on gustatory adjectives, where vision precedes hearing on the synaesthetic hierarchy for Mandarin gustatory adjectives, while vision follows hearing on the synaesthetic hierarchy for English gustatory adjectives. Based on Mandarin sensory adjectives with more than one sensory meaning in 现代汉语词典 *Xian4-dai4 han4-yu3 ci2-dian3* 'Contemporary Chinese Dictionary', Zhao and Huang (2018) generalized a synaesthetic hierarchy for Mandarin sensory adjectives.[3] The research has shown that the general transfer hierarchy of Mandarin synaesthesia is different from that of English synaesthesia in accordance with Williams (1976). For example, touch and taste could be source domains for each other for transfers of linguistic synaesthesia in Mandarin (Zhao and Huang 2018), while there is a unidirectional transfer from touch to taste in linguistic synaesthesia in English (Williams 1976). In addition, Zhao and Huang (2018) proposed that the salience of sensory modalities in the human sensory system, in addition to physical contact, is also a factor that motivates the transfer directions of linguistic synaesthesia. Following this proposal, vision and hearing are more salient and thus more embodied than smell, which could explain why smell is the least productive source domain on the highest position in the transfer hierarchy of Mandarin synaesthesia (Zhao and Huang 2018). Although these studies have established that Mandarin shows language-specific characteristics in linguistic synaesthesia, one limitation is the relatively small sample of synaesthetic examples employed. They tend to be based either on linguistic synaesthesia for specific lexical items and sensory domains (e.g., Xiong and Huang 2015; Zhao and Huang 2015; Zhao et al. 2018b) or on synaesthetic adjectives from the dictionary (e.g., Zhao and Huang 2018). Thus, a large-scale empirical data set derived from corpora is still needed for a comprehensive description of the general tendencies of Mandarin synaesthesia.

Another perspective from the research on Chinese synaesthesia is the examination of the distributions and grammatical functions of linguistic synaesthesia in Chinese. Studies such as Xiong and Huang (2016) and Huang and Xiong (2019) have shown that linguistic synaesthesia can occur not only in diverse genres of Chinese texts (e.g., poems, novels, Chinese translation texts of Buddhism, and ordinary Mandarin), but it can also function in multiple levels of Chinese including semantic compositions of Chinese characters, words, and phrases.

Zhao et al. (2019) have demonstrated that linguistic synaesthesia shows systematic distributions in both poetic and non-poetic Chinese. In addition, the study suggested that linguistic synaesthesia in general, and linguistic synaesthesia of Chinese in particular, could yield significant results from both the linguistic and the inter-disciplinary perspectives. For instance, linguistic synaesthesia in Chinese showing language-specific characteristics would pose a challenge to the hypothesis of the cross-linguistic universality of transfer tendencies for linguistic synaesthesia in human languages (Zhao et al. 2019). Linguistic synaesthesia showing

---

[3]Sensory adjectives employed by Zhao and Huang (2018) have their different sensory meanings differentiated into distinct sememe entries in the dictionary, which are thus so-called polysemous words. By contrast, this study will utilize a larger sample of Mandarin sensory adjectives, which show distributions in different sensory modalities in the corpus rather than are annotated as polysemous with respect to sensory meanings in the dictionary. For more information about polysemy of perception items, please see Ibarretxe-Antuñano (1999).

directionality tendencies grounded in both embodied and neural mechanisms could provide implications for the embodiment theory in cognitive science and for neurological synaesthesia in brain science (Zhao et al. 2019).

It is noteworthy that Mandarin Chinese, as a Sino-Tibetan language (Chen 1999), is typologically distinct from Indo-European languages, Hebrew, and Indonesian. A systematic and comprehensive study on linguistic synaesthesia in Mandarin Chinese would establish more meaningful correlations between linguistic behaviors in general and theoretical accounts for linguistic synaesthesia in human languages. Strik Lievers (2015) and Winter (2016a) have found that linguistic synaesthesia is productive in sensory adjectives.[4] Thus, this study will also focus on synaesthetic expressions of sensory adjectives in Mandarin Chinese. Based on the distributions of Mandarin synaesthetic adjectives (i.e., adjectives used for more than one sensory domain in Mandarin) in the corpus, this book aims to explore general tendencies and theoretical explanations for Mandarin synaesthesia. In addition, it also seeks to clarify the nature of linguistic synaesthesia and provide theoretical implications for CMT based on patterns of linguistic synaesthesia in Mandarin Chinese.

1.3 Research Issues

The review of the literature elaborated above shows that there are notable gaps in the research on linguistic synaesthesia at two levels. One is related to linguistic synaesthesia in human languages in general, and the other is linguistic synaesthesia in Mandarin Chinese in particular.

With respect to general research gaps concerning linguistic synaesthesia in the literature, few implications have been provided to support or disprove the two rival theoretical accounts for mechanisms underlying linguistic synaesthesia. That is because previous studies on linguistic synaesthesia in Indo-European languages (e.g., English, Italian, and French) and non-Indo-European languages (e.g., Hebrew and Indonesian) have shown similar transfer patterns for linguistic synaesthesia. Therefore, neither the directionality of linguistic synaesthesia mapping from the more embodied to the less embodied predicted by the embodiment account, nor the cross-linguistic universality of synaesthetic patterns in human languages assumed by the biological association account, can be confuted. On the other hand, both explanatory models can only account for a part of synaesthetic uses when taken into consideration exclusively (Zhao et al. 2018b). Thus, more and finer-grained constructs are needed for both the theoretical models if adopted.

[4] A more recent study, Strik Lievers and Winter (2018), has found that different sensory modalities are encoded differently across lexical categories, including nouns, verbs, and adjectives in English. Thus, it would be interesting to examine whether linguistic synaesthesia used frequently among adjectives, rather than among verbs or nouns, is related to the lexical patterns of human senses. The book leaves the issue for future research.

These general research gaps can be addressed by examining more comprehensive data covering typologically diverse languages. Mandarin Chinese, as a member of the Sino-Tibetan language family (Chen 1999), is a good candidate, as it is typologically distinct from Indo-European languages and from non-Indo-European languages including Hebrew and Indonesian.

The research gaps for Mandarin synaesthesia in particular lie in both transfer patterns and theoretical explanations. As demonstrated in Sect. 1.2, previous studies on linguistic synaesthesia in Mandarin Chinese are mostly based on a small sample of data. Thus, the assumptions that Mandarin synaesthesia shows language-specific characteristics for directional tendencies and that Mandarin synaesthesia is grounded in both embodied and neural mechanisms need to be tested through more comprehensive and systematic data.

To summarize, research questions this book aims to address include:

(1) What tendencies does linguistic synaesthesia in Mandarin Chinese show, when a large-scale sample of synaesthetic data considered?
(2) Does linguistic synaesthesia in Mandarin show the same tendencies as it does in Indo-European languages? In other words, is linguistic synaesthesia subject to cultural differences or not?
(3) What mechanisms underlie Mandarin synaesthesia?
(4) Which theoretical model best explains the tendencies of Mandarin synaesthesia?
(5) What is the nature of linguistic synaesthesia, based on patterns of Mandarin synaesthesia?
(6) What theoretical implications does linguistic synaesthesia provide for CMT and the theory of embodiment?

1.4 Overview of the Book

Chapter 2 will propose a linguistic synaesthesia identification procedure (LSIP) to extract Mandarin synaesthetic adjectives, based on which data collection and analysis will be elaborated. In this chapter, I will also present an overview of the extracted synaesthetic data, to give a brief demonstration showing that sensory associations between different modalities in Mandarin expressions (i.e., Mandarin synaesthesia) are not random, but instead conform to certain patterns.

Chapters 3 and 4 will focus on transfer patterns and underlying mechanisms of linguistic synaesthesia in Mandarin tactile and gustatory adjectives respectively, as touch and taste are the two most predominant sensory modalities for source domains in linguistic synaesthesia based on the collected Mandarin synaesthetic data. In these two chapters, I will show that although the embodiment account predicts most synaesthetic transfers of Mandarin tactile and gustatory adjectives, there are notable synaesthetic uses of the adjectives that support the biological association account. In addition, these two chapters will establish that linguistic synaesthesia in Mandarin tactile and gustatory adjectives can be grounded in multiple mechanisms, including perceived similarity, sensory integration, and biological association. Another interesting pattern discussed in the chapters is that the unidirectional transfer from touch to taste reported in linguistic synaesthetic expressions in Indo-European languages cannot be attested in Mandarin. Rather, Mandarin synaesthesia shows a bidirectionality between touch and taste.

Chapter 5 will discuss linguistic synaesthetic expressions in Mandarin visual, auditory, and olfactory adjectives, as vision, hearing, and smell act as source domains less frequently than touch and taste in Mandarin synaesthesia. Moreover, given that Shen (1997) suggested that vision, hearing, and smell are less embodied than touch and taste, Chap. 5 will not only test the assumption of the higher degree of embodiment of tactile and gustatory sensations among five senses, but also establish the embodiment degrees among vision, hearing, and smell based on tendencies in Mandarin synaesthesia.

Chapter 6 will present additional evidence to support the theory that Mandarin synaesthesia exhibits directional tendencies and human senses manifest themselves with different degrees of embodiment, by focusing on the synaesthetic patterns of Mandarin compound adjectives combining different sensory modalities.

Chapter 7 will determine the theoretical implications of linguistic synaesthesia, where I will propose an incorporated theoretical model to account for linguistic synaesthesia. In this chapter, I will also clarify the metaphorical nature of linguistic synaesthesia. In other words, linguistic synaesthesia is also an embodied conceptualization, as the same as canonical metaphors. Furthermore, I will argue for a finer-grained account of embodiment covering the notions of the degree of embodiment and the type of embodied events, which should be included by CMT and the embodiment theory.

Chapter 8 will summarize the findings of this study and propose future work.

References

Ahrens, Kathleen. 2002. When love is not digested: Underlying reasons for source to target domain pairings in the contemporary theory of metaphor. In *Proceedings of the first Cognitive Linguistics Conference*, 273–302.

Asano, Michiko, and Kazuhiko Yokosawa. 2012. Synesthetic colors for Japanese late acquired graphemes. *Consciousness and Cognition* 21: 983–993.

Banissy, Michael, Clare Jonas, and Roi Cohen Kadosh. 2014. Synesthesia: An introduction. *Frontiers in Psychology* 5(1414): 1–3.

Banissy, Michael, Roi Cohen Kadosh, and Clare Jonas (eds.). 2015. *Synaesthesia*. Lausanne: Frontiers Media.

Baroni, Marco, Silvia Bernardini, Adriano Ferraresi, and Eros Zanchetta. 2009. The WaCky wide web: A collection of very large linguistically processed web-crawled corpora. *Language Resources and Evaluation* 43(3): 209–226.

Caballero, Rosario, and Carita Paradis. 2015. Making sense of sensory perceptions across languages and cultures. *Functions of Language* 22(1): 1–19.

Cacciari, Cristina. 2008. Crossing the senses in metaphorical language. In *The Cambridge handbook of metaphor and thought*, ed. Raymond Gibbs, 425–443. New York: Cambridge University Press.

Caterina, Michael, Mark Schumacher, Makoto Tominaga, Tobias Rosen, Jon Levine, and David Julius. 1997. The capsaicin receptor: A heat-activated ion channel in the pain pathway. *Nature* 389(6653): 816–824.

Chen, Baoya (陈保亚). 1999. *Chinese linguistics methodology in the 20th century: 1898–1998* [二十世纪中国语言学方法论:1898-1998]. Jinan [济南]: Shangdong Education Press [山东教育出版社].

Chen, Keh-Jiann, Chu-Ren Huang, Li-Ping Chang and Hui-Li Hsu. 1996. Sinica corpus: Design methodology for balanced corpora. In *Proceedings of the 11th Pacific Asia Conference on Language, Information and Computation (PACLIC 11)*, 167–176.

Chung, Siaw-Fong (钟晓芳), Kathleen Ahrens (安可思) and Chu-Ren Huang (黄居仁). 2013. Ontologies and conceptual metaphors in English and Mandarin [中英知识本体与概念隐喻]. *Contemporary Linguistics* [当代语言学] 2: 195–213.

Chu-Ren, Huang, and Jiajuan Xiong. 2019. Linguistic synaesthesia in Chinese. In *The Routledge handbook of applied chinese linguistics*, ed. Chu-Ren Huang, Zhuo Jing-Schmidt, and Barbara Meisterernst, 294–312. London: Routledge.

Clausner, Timothy C., and William Croft. 1999. Domains and image schemas. *Cognitive Linguistics* 10(1): 1–31.

Cytowic, Richard. 1993. *The man who tasted shapes: A bizarre medical mystery offers revolutionary insights into emotions, reasoning and consciousness*. New York: G. P. Putnam's.

Cytowic, Richard. 2002 [1989]. *Synesthesia: A union of the senses* (2nd ed.). Cambridge: The MIT Press.

Day, Sean. 1996. Synaesthesia and synaesthetic metaphors. *Psyche* 2(32): 1–16.

Gardner, Howard. 1974. Metaphors and modalities: How children project polar adjectives onto diverse domains. *Child Development* 45(1): 84–91.

Geeraerts, Dirk. 2010. *Theories of lexical semantics*. Oxford and New York: Oxford University Press.

Gibbs, Raymond W. 2011. Evaluating conceptual metaphor theory. *Discourse Processes* 48(8): 529–562.

Grady, Joseph. 2005. Primary metaphors as inputs to conceptual integration. *Journal of Pragmatics* 37(10): 1595–1614.

Hubbard, Edward, and Vilayanur Ramachandran. 2005. Neurocognitive mechanisms of synesthesia. *Neuron* 48(3): 509–520.

Hung, Wan-Yu., Julia Simner, Richard Shillcock, and David M. Eagleman. 2014. Synesthesia in Chinese characters: The role of radical function and position. *Consciousness and Cognition* 24: 38–48.

Ibarretxe-Antuñano, Iraide. 1999. *Polysemy and metaphor in perception verbs: A cross-linguistic study*. Ph.D. thesis. University of Edinburgh.

Johnson, Mark. 1987. *The body in the mind: The bodily basis of meaning, imagination, and reason*. Chicago: University of Chicago Press.

Keil, Frank C. 1986. Conceptual domains and the acquisition of metaphor. *Cognitive Development* 1(1): 73–96.

Lakoff, George, and Mark Johnson. 1980. *Metaphors we live by*. Chicago: University of Chicago Press.

Lakoff, George, and Mark Johnson. 1999. *Philosophy in the flesh: The embodied mind and its challenge to Western thought*. New York: Basic Books.

Lehrer, Adrienne. 1978. Structures of the lexicon and transfer of meaning. *Lingua* 45(2): 95–123.

Li, Guonan (李国南). 1996. The physiological commonality of synaesthesia [论"通感"的人类生理学共性]. *Journal of Foreign Language* [外国语(上海外国语大学学报)] 3: 34–40.

Lien, Chinfa. 1994. Synaesthetic words in the Southern Min dialect: Their semantic structure and change. In *Chinese Languages and Linguistics*, vol. 2, ed. Paul Jen-kuei Li, Chu-Ren Huang, and Chih-Chen Jan Tang, 421–451. Historical Linguistics Taipei: Institute of History and Philology, Academia Sinica.

Lien, Chinfa. 2005. Verbs of visual perception in Taiwanese Southern Min: A cognitive approach to shift of semantic domains. *Language and Linguistics* 6(1): 109–132.

Marks, Lawrence, and Catherine Mulvenna. 2013. Synesthesia, at and near its borders. *Frontiers in Psychology* 4(651): 1–4.

Marks, Lawrence, Robin Hammeal, Marc Bornstein, and Linda Smith. 1987. Perceiving similarity and comprehending metaphor. *Monographs of the Society for Research in Child Development* 52(1): 1–100.

Osgood, Charles, George Suci and Percy Tannenbaum. 1978 [1957]. *The measurement of meaning* (4th ed.). Urbana, Chicago and London: University of Illinois Press.

Ou, Te-Fen (欧德芬). 2014. A cognitive study of the senses of the Chinese polysemous verb 'kan' [多义感官动词"看"义项之认知研究]. *Language and Linguistics* [语言暨语言学] 15(2): 159–198.

Paradis, Carita. 2001. Adjectives and boundedness. *Cognitive Linguistics* 12(1): 47–64.

Peng, Yi (彭懿) and Jiehong Bai (白解红). 2008. A new perspective to the linguistic synaesthesia [通感认知新论]. *Foreign Languages and Their Teaching* [外语与外语教学] 1(1): 14–17.

Popova, Yanna. 2005. Image schemas and verbal synaesthesia. In *From perception to meaning: Image schema in cognitive linguistics (cognitive linguistics research 29)*, ed. Beate Hampe and Joseph Grady, 395–420. Berlin and New York: Mouton de Gruyter.

Qian, Zhongshu (钱钟书). 1985. Synaesthesia [通感], *Seven pieces patched together* [七缀集], 54–66. Shanghai [上海]: Shanghai Classics Publishing House [上海古籍出版社].

Rakova, Marina. 2003. *The extent of the literal: Metaphor, polysemy and the theories of concepts*. Hampshire: Palgrave Macmillan.

Ramachandran, Vilayanur, and Edward Hubbard. 2001. Synaesthesia—A window into perception, thought and language. *Journal of Consciousness Studies* 8(12): 3–34.

Ronga, Irene, Carla Bazzanella, Ferdinando Rossi, and Giandomenico Iannetti. 2012. Linguistic synaesthesia, perceptual synaesthesia, and the interaction between multiple sensory modalities. *Pragmatics & Cognition* 20(1): 135–167.

Seitz, Jay. 1997. The development of metaphoric understanding: Implications for a theory of creativity. *Creativity Research Journal* 10(4): 347–353.

Seitz, Jay. 2005. The neutral, evolutionary, developmental, and bodily basis of metaphor. *New Ideas in Psychology* 23(2): 74–95.

Shen, Yeshayahu. 1997. Cognitive constraints on poetic figures. *Cognitive Linguistics* 8(1): 33–71.

Shen, Yeshayahu, and Michal Cohen. 1998. How come silence is sweet but sweetness is not silent: A cognitive account of directionality in poetic synaesthesia. *Language and Literature* 7(2): 123–140.

Shen, Yeshayahu, and David Eisenman. 2008. "Heard melodies are sweet, but those unheard are sweeter": Synaesthesia and cognition. *Language and Literature* 17(2): 101–121.

Shen, Yeshayahu, and Osnat Gadir. 2009. How to interpret the music of caressing: Target and source assignment in synaesthetic genitive constructions. *Journal of Pragmatics* 41(2): 357–371.

Shen, Yeshayahu, and David Gil. 2008. Sweet fragrances from Indonesia: A universal principle governing directionality in synaesthetic metaphors. In *New beginnings in literary studies*, ed. Jan Auracher and Willie van Peer, 49–71. Newcastle: Cambridge Scholars Publishing.

Simner, Julia, and Edward Hubbard (eds.). 2013. *The Oxford handbook of synesthesia*. Oxford: Oxford University Press.

Steen, Gerard. 1999. From linguistic to conceptual metaphor in five steps. In *Metaphor in Cognitive Linguistics: Selected Papers from the 5th International Cognitive Linguistics Conference*, eds. Raymond W. Gibbs and Gerard J. Steen, 57–77. Amsterdam and Philadelphia: John Benjamins Publishing Company.

Strik Lievers, Francesca. 2015. Synaesthesia: A corpus-based study of cross-modal directionality. *Functions of Language* 22(1): 69–95.

Strik Lievers, Francesca. 2017. Figures and the senses: Towards a definition of synaesthesia. *Review of Cognitive Linguistics* 15(1): 83–101.

Strik Lievers, Francesca, and Bodo Winter. 2018. Sensory language across categories. *Lingua* 204: 45–61.

Sweetser, Eve. 1990. *From etymology to pragmatics: Metaphorical and cultural aspects of semantic structure*. Cambridge and New York: Cambridge University Press.

Ullmann, Stephen. 1945. Romanticism and synaesthesia: A comparative study of sense transfer in Keats and Byron. *Publications of the Modern Language Association of America* 60(3): 811–827.

Ullmann, Stephen. 1957. *The principles of semantics*. Oxford: Basil Blackwell.

Ullmann, Stephen. 1966 [1963]. Semantic universals. In *Universals of language* (2nd ed.), ed. Joseph Greenberg, 217–262. Cambridge and London: The MIT Press.

Viberg, Åke. 1983. The verbs of perception: A typological study. *Linguistics* 21(1): 123–162.

Wang, Shaohua (汪少华). 2002. Synaesethesia, association and cognition [通感•联想•认知]. *Modern Foreign Languages* [现代外语] 25(2): 187–194.

Wang, Shaohua (汪少华) and Jian Xu (徐健). 2002. Synaesthesia and conceptual metaphor [通感与概念隐喻]. *Foreign Language Research* [外语学刊] 3: 91–94.

Wang, Yuhong (王宇弘). 2008. The cognitive foundation and philosophical implication of synaesthetic metaphors [通感隐喻的认知基础和哲学意义]. *Foreign Language and Their Teaching* [外语与外语教学] 4(1): 13–16.

Ward, Jamie, Brett Huckstep, and Elias Tsakanikos. 2006. Sound-colour synaesthesia: To what extent does it use cross-modal mechanisms common to us all? *Cortex* 42(2): 264–280.

Williams, Joseph. 1976. Synaesthetic adjectives: A possible law of sematic change. *Language* 52 (2): 461–478.

Winter, Bodo. 2016a. *The sensory structure of the English lexicon*. Merced, CA: University of California, Merced dissertation.

Winter, Bodo. 2019a. *Sensory linguistics: Language, perception and metaphor*. Amsterdam and Philadelphia: John Benjamins Publishing Company.

Winter, Bodo. 2019b. Synaesthetic metaphors are neither synaesthetic nor metaphorical. In *Perception metaphors*, ed. Laura J. Speed, Carolyn O'Meara, Lila San Roque, and Asifa Majid, 105–126. Amsterdam and Philadelphia: John Benjamins Publishing Company.

Xiong, Jiajuan and Chu-Ren Huang. 2015. Being assiduous: Do we have BITTERNESS or PAIN? The synaesthetic and conceptual metaphors of BITTERNESS and PAIN in Chinese and English. In *Chinese lexical semantics* (LNAI 9332), eds. Qin Lu and Helena Hong Gao, 15–23. Gewerbestrasse: Springer International Publishing.

Xiong, Jiajuan and Chu-Ren Huang. 2016. The synaesthetic and metaphorical uses of 味 *wei4* 'taste'. In *Proceedings of the 30th Pacific Asia Conference on Language, Information and Computation (PACLIC-30)*, 485–492.

Yang, Bo (杨波) and Hui Zhang (张辉). 2007. Cross-modal perception and synaesthetic adjectives [跨感官感知与通感形容词研究]. *Foreign Language Education* [外语教学] 28(1): 16–21.

Yu, Ning. 2003. Synesthetic metaphors: A cognitive perspective. *Journal of Literary Semantics* 32 (1): 19–34.

Zhao, Qingqing, and Chu-Ren Huang. 2015. A corpus-based study on synaesthetic adjectives in Modern Chinese. In *Chinese lexical semantics (LNAI 9332)*, ed. Qin Lu and Helena Hong Gao, 535–542. Gewerbestrasse: Springer International Publishing.

Zhao, Qingqing (赵青青) and Chu-Ren Huang (黄居仁). 2018. Mapping models and underlying mechanisms of synaesthetic metaphors in Mandarin [现代汉语通感隐喻的映射模型与制约机制]. *Language Teaching and Linguistic Studies* [语言教学与研究] 1: 44–55.

Zhao, Qingqing (赵青青), Jiajuan Xiong (熊佳娟) and Chu-Ren Huang (黄居仁). 2019. Linguistic synaesthesia, metaphor, and cognition: The systematicity and significance of linguistic synaesthesia in Chinese [通感、隐喻与认知——通感现象在汉语中的系统性表现与语言学价值]. *Zhuoguoyuwen* [中国语文] 2: 240–253.

Zhao, Qingqing, Chu-Ren Huang and Hongzhi Xu. 2015. Auditory synaesthesia and near synonyms: A corpus-based analysis of sheng1 and yin1 in Mandarin Chinese. In *Proceedings of the 29th Pacific Asia Conference on Language, Information and Computation (PACLIC-29)*, 315–322.

Zhao, Qingqing, Chu-Ren Huang, and Yunfei Long. 2018b. Synaesthesia in Chinese: A corpus-based study on gustatory adjectives in Mandarin. *Linguistics* 56(5): 1167–1194.

Chapter 2
Methodology: A Corpus-Driven Approach

The distinction between corpus-based and corpus-driven approaches in Corpus Linguistics has been questioned, as they show few differences in methodology (Meyer 2014). However, various studies have recognized distinct theoretical tenets underlying the two approaches. Corpus-based research aims to validate a specific theory through corpus data, while corpus-driven research has no pre-defined linguistic theories, but rather arrives at explanatory theories through an analysis of corpus data (Biber 2012; Meyer 2014; among others). As there are no pre-defined theories, per se, for Mandarin linguistic synaesthesia, this book focuses on a systematic and comprehensive corpus-driven study on Mandarin synaesthetic adjectives to examine the general tendencies and underlying mechanisms of linguistic synaesthesia.

This chapter will elaborate on the methodology of Mandarin synaesthesia data collection from a balanced corpus, i.e., the Sinica corpus.[1] The analysis of collected synaesthetic data will be shown for transfer directions of Mandarin synaesthesia as well. Specifically, Sect. 2.1 will propose a linguistic synaesthesia identification procedure (LSIP) to extract synaesthetic uses of Mandarin sensory adjectives in the corpus. The procedure includes three parts: (1) identification of basic sensory meanings of Mandarin sensory adjectives, (2) classification of human sensory modalities, and (3) collection of synaesthetic expressions from the Sinica corpus. Section 2.2 will present an overview of the extracted synaesthetic data based on LSIP. I will summarize data distributions in the Sinica corpus of Mandarin synaesthetic adjectives, and make generalizations on synaesthetic participation rates

[1]The Sinica corpus (The Academia Sinica Balanced Corpus) is a balanced corpus for Modern Chinese with part-of-speech tagging (see Chen et al. 1996). The version used in the current study (i.e., the 4th edition) contains ten million word tokens, which can be accessed at http://lingcorpus.iis.sinica.edu.tw/modern/.

Q. Zhao, *Embodied Conceptualization or Neural Realization*,
Frontiers in Chinese Linguistics 10, https://doi.org/10.1007/978-981-32-9315-1_2

of Mandarin sensory adjectives from five senses as well as sensory associations in Mandarin synaesthetic adjectives. The last section will summarize the content of this chapter.

2.1 A Linguistic Synaesthesia Identification Procedure

Linguistic synaesthesia involves the mapping of a concept from the source domain to the target domain, just like in other types of metaphor (e.g., Shen 1997; Yu 2003). Hence, it is reasonable to assume that established procedures for the identification of metaphors can be adapted for the identification of linguistic synaesthesia.[2]. This study thus adopted and modified the well-established metaphor identification procedure (MIP) proposed by Pragglejaz Group (2007) and its updated version (i.e., MIPVU), extended by Steen et al. (2010), to identify synaesthetic usages of Mandarin sensory adjectives in the Sinica corpus.[3]

For the identification of metaphors in both MIP and MIPVU, one must determine whether a lexical item "has a more basic contemporary meaning in other contexts than the one in the given context" (Pragglejaz Group 2007: 3). The basic meanings of lexical items are assumed to be generally "more concrete" (i.e., the evoked entities are easier to imagine, see, hear, feel, smell, and taste), "related to bodily action", "more precise", and "historically older" (Pragglejaz Group 2007: 3).[4] With respect to linguistic synaesthesia, both the source domain and the target domain are embodied and concrete sensory modalities (Shen 1997; Yu 2003). Thus, linguistic synaesthesia poses a challenge to MIP and MIPVU in determining which contemporary sensory usage of a lexical item is more basic. In other words, except for the historical information, meanings in source domains and in target domains for sensory items in linguistic synaesthesia would not be likely to show sharp differences concerning concreteness, relatedness to bodily actions, or preciseness.

[2]Please note that LSIP can be adapted from the identification procedures for metaphors, as linguistic synaesthesia shares the same characteristic with canonical metaphors with respect to mappings of concepts from one domain to another domain. Nevertheless, it is still arguable whether linguistic synaesthesia is a kind of metaphor or not by its very nature, since linguistic synaesthesia does show differences from prototypical metaphors, including, for instance, the contrast of embodiment between source domains and target domains, and directional tendencies of mappings (see Sect. 1.1.3).

[3]A variety of applications and extensions of the metaphor identification procedure by Pragglejaz Group (2007) and Steen et al. (2010) can be found in the literature. For instance, Semino's (2010) study based the description of English pain metaphors on the procedure, and Burgers et al. (2011) extended the procedure to identify verbal irony in discourse. For the identification procedure of conceptual metaphors specifically, please see Steen (1999).

[4]Please note that the basic meanings are not assumed to be equal to the frequent or common meanings for lexical items by Pragglejaz Group (2007). This study mainly relies on the historically older meanings to determine the basic meanings for lexical items in connection with sensory modalities. More details will be given in Sect. 2.1.1.

Therefore, in order to adapt MIP and MIPVU for the identification of linguistic synaesthesia, one key point is to find feasible criteria to determine the basic sensory meanings of sensory words.

2.1.1 Identification of Basic Sensory Meanings

Using citation dates in dictionaries, Williams (1976) concluded that the earliest cited sensory meaning of a sensory word is its basic sensory meaning, and that the basic sensory meaning's sensory modality is the source domain of synaesthetic transfers for that sensory word. Relying on this kind of evidence exclusively has been criticized (see Lehrer 1978), so this study made use of multiple linguistic clues to ensure more reliable decisions on the basic sensory meanings and source domains for Mandarin sensory adjectives.

Firstly, I considered both the etymological origins of sensory items in Chinese etymological dictionaries and specific uses of these items in Classic Chinese (particularly in pre-Qin texts) to ensure that the correct etymology was identified. Specifically, I consulted both 说文解字 *Shuo1-wen2 jie3-zi4* 'Explaining Graphs and Analyzing Characters' (Xu 1963 [156]) and 说文解字注 *Shuo1-wen2 jie3-zi4 zhu4* 'Commentary on Explaining Graphs and Analyzing Characters' (Duan 2007 [1735–1815]), two well-established Chinese etymology dictionaries available through the online interface of 汉典 *Han4-dian3* 'Zdic.net'.[5] In addition, 汉语大字典 *Han4-yu3 da4 zi4-dian3* 'Great Compendium of Chinese Characters' (Xu 2010 [1986]) was also consulted to double-check the original meanings of sensory items and to identify the original meanings of sensory items that are not included in 说文解字 *Shuo1-wen2 jie3-zi4* and 说文解字注 *Shuo1-wen2 jie3-zi4 zhu4*. In terms of earlier usages of sensory items in Classic Chinese, I referred to the Classic Chinese database of 汉达文库 *Han4-da2 wen2-ku4* 'Chinese Ancient Texts Database (CHANT)' (D.C. Lau Research Centre 2005).[6]

It is important to note that philological information from Chinese characters themselves can also provide etymological evidence for lexical items (Wang 1996; Huang and Hsieh 2015). Thus, this study also relied on the philological information from Chinese characters to figure out the basic sensory meanings of Mandarin sensory adjectives. For example, the radical 舌 'tongue' in the Mandarin adjective 甜 *tian2* 'sweet' (see Xu 1963 [156]) can be considered an additional piece of evidence, to indicate the gustatory origin of the adjective etymologically, since the

[5]汉典 *Han4-dian3* 'Zdic.net'is a free online thesaurus with paraphrases of more than 90,000 Chinese characters from well-established Chinese dictionaries, which can be accessed at: http://www.zdic.net/.

[6]The CHANT database consists of six traditional and excavated ancient Chinese texts databases: Jiaguwen Database, Jianbo Database, Jinwen Database, Pre-Han and Han Transmitted Texts Database, Six Dynasties Transmitted Texts Database, and Chinese Traditional Leishu Database, which can be accessed at: http://www.chant.org/.

radical conceptualizes the sensory organ which humans normally use to obtain gustatory perceptions. It should be noted that the glyphic composition information of Chinese characters is an orthographical rule, rather than necessarily lexical representations of lexical units. Nevertheless, the conceptual motivation of the radical in a specific lexical unit would provide a commonly accepted way to conventionalize the basic meaning of the unit, as suggested in various Chinese philological studies, such as Xu (1963 [156]), Wang (1996), and Huang and Hsieh (2015). To put it differently, the original meaning of the lexical unit would be the most likely to be equal to or closely related to the conceptual motivation of the radical. In this study, the philological information from characters was employed together with other evidence, rather than exclusively, to attest to an adjective's etymology, which would thus enhance the likelihood of identifying the correct etymology for Mandarin sensory words. Take the Mandarin adjective 美 *mei3* for example, which is composed of 羊 'sheep' and 大 'big', where the former glyph conceptualizes an edible object and the latter a visual perception (Xu 1963 [156]). The original meaning of the adjective was paraphrased as 'tasty' in 说文解字 *Shuo1-wen2 jie3-zi4*, and one of its uses in pre-Qin texts is 脍炙与羊枣孰美 *kuai4-zhi4 yu3 yang2-zao3 shu2 mei3* 'which is more tasty, the toasted shredded meat, or the black oval jujube?' in 孟子 *Meng4-zi3* (around the 3rd century BC). Therefore, together with the paraphrasing and the earlier usage, the gustatory concept of the character could be more basic than the visual concept. It is thus concluded that the adjective 美 *mei3* has an original meaning of 'tasty' (taste) but later was developed the meaning of 'beautiful' (vision) through linguistic synaesthesia. In general, this study relied on the online interface of Hantology (Chou and Huang 2010) for the philological information of Chinese characters.[7]

The etymological origins of some Mandarin sensory words cannot be determined on the basis of the information in historical texts or on the orthographical composition of Chinese characters. For example, the adjective 浓 *nong2* describes both intense taste (taste), such as 浓茶 *nong2 cha2* 'strong tea', and intense color (vision), such as 浓绿 *nong2 lv4* 'deep green' in Mandarin. The two usages correspond to 醲 *nong2* 'strong wine' and 濃 *nong2* 'dense dew' in 说文解字 *Shuo1-wen2 jie3-zi4* respectively. Thus, the gustatory modality and the visual modality are both possible source domains for the adjective 浓 *nong2* in linguistic synaesthesia. However, 浓 *nong2* shows a close relation with the adjective 淡 *dan4* 'not salty/of mild taste' in Mandarin, both in meaning (i.e., antonymy) and in orthography (i.e., with the radical conceptualizing 'water'). This study thus assumes that 浓 *nong2* and 淡 *dan4* should belong to the same sensory modality originally. With respect to the etymology of 淡 *dan4*, its gustatory origin can be attested clearly, as it has the paraphrasing of 'thin taste' in 说文解字 *Shuo1-wen2 jie3-zi4*, and one of its earlier uses is 甘苦咸淡辛酸奇味以口异 *gan1 ku3 xian2 dan4 xin1 suan1 qi2-wei4 yi3 kou3 yi4* 'sweetness, bitterness, the salty taste, the mild taste, the hot taste, sourness, and the special taste are differentiated by the mouth' in 荀子 *Xun2-zi3* (around the

[7]The interface of Hantology can be accessed at: http://hantology.ling.sinica.edu.tw/.

3rd century BC). Therefore, 浓 *nong2* was assigned to the gustatory domain with the basic sensory meaning as 'of intense taste'. Through this comparison analysis, all sensory items without explicit etymological evidence for the source domains in linguistic synaesthesia were assigned a specific basic sensory meaning in this study.

Another challenging issue, concerning identification of the basic sensory meanings for Mandarin sensory adjectives, is related to compound words. In principle, this study relied on the etymological meanings of constituent morphemes to determine the basic sensory domains of compound words. Specifically, Mandarin sensory compounds comprising morphemes with the same etymology with respect to the sensory modality are considered to have the same basic sensory domains as their constituent morphemes. Sensory words composed of morphemes from different sensory modalities have been annotated as combinations of different sensory modalities. For instance, 甘甜 *gan1-tian2* 'sweet' was determined to have taste as its basic sensory domain, since both 甘 *gan1* 'sweet' and 甜 *tian2* 'sweet' are gustatory items originally, while 苦涩 *ku3-se4* 'bitter' was annotated as 'TASTE + TOUCH', based on the gustatory origin of 苦 *ku3* 'bitter vegetable' and the tactile origin of 涩 *se4* 'not flowing smoothly' etymologically.

When dealing with compounds that combine different sensory modalities, it is important to consider that some sensory words involve linguistic synaesthesia within the word boundary, and these compounds are concerned with one single sense (Huang and Xiong 2019). Take the Mandarin sensory adjective 鲜艳 *xian1-yan4* 'bright in colors' for example: 鲜 *xian1*, originally meaning 'a kind of fish', underwent a synaesthetic transfer from taste to vision, and the whole compound relates to that single sense (i.e., vision), the same one as the original domain of 艳 *yan4* 'bright in colors'. Other sensory adjectives composed of morphemes with different sensory origins, however, are juxtapositions of different sensory morphemes, and these compounds denote more than one piece of sensory information. For example, the Mandarin adjective 细软 *xi4-ruan3* means 'thin and soft' as in the phrase 细软的头发 *xi4-ruan3 de tou2-fa4* 'the thin and soft hair', which evokes both vision and touch. This book focuses on the synaesthetic uses of Mandarin sensory adjectives, and it will not explore linguistic synaesthesia in semantic compositions of words in depth. It is sufficient to annotate the combination patterns of different senses for sensory adjectives consisting of morphemes with distinct sensory origins. In other words, these adjectives are considered to have synaesthetic uses if they describe senses unrelated to the senses in their constituent morphemes. For instance, 苦涩 *ku3-se4* 'bitter' in the expression 苦涩的异国香味 *ku3-se4 de yi4-guo2 xiang1wei4* 'the bitter and exotic fragrance' was identified as a synaesthetic usage, as it was employed to describe an olfactory perception, hence involving neither taste nor touch, the categories to which the constituent morphemes belong.

To summarize, this study has relied on multiple linguistic clues to identify the basic sensory meanings for Mandarin sensory adjectives, which include the etymological origins paraphrased in Chinese etymology dictionaries, earlier usages of sensory items in Classic Chinese texts, philological composition information of Chinese characters, and comparison analyses between attested items and unattested items.

It should be noted that the basic sensory meanings of Mandarin sensory adjectives identified in this study are not always the same as, and not necessarily equal to, the most accessible sensory meanings of the adjectives. For example, the Mandarin adjective 美 *mei3* is used much more frequently for vision (1222 tokens) than for taste (182 tokens) based on the Sinica corpus. The visual meaning is also generally more accessible than the gustatory meaning of the adjective 美 *mei3* for native speakers of Mandarin. However, according to the etymology of the adjective, the gustatory meaning is more likely the basic sensory meaning of the adjective, as the diachronic directions of meaning extensions are more important for this study to determine transfer directions of linguistic synaesthesia.

There have been studies employing experimental methods to determine the accessibility of the sensory concepts encoded in sensory items. For instance, Lynott and Connell (2009) and Lynott and Connell (2013) asked participants to rate the perceptual strengths of English sensory words in five sensory modalities (i.e., touch, taste, vision, hearing, and smell). Chen et al. (2019) utilized a similar rating task for Mandarin sensory words. As predicted by Winter (2016a), specific sensory words can be assigned different basic sensory meanings depending on the method of analysis: an experimental method on conceptual accessibility versus a diachronic approach based on lexical etymology. For instance, Mandarin adjective 涩 *se4* 'not flowing smoothly' has been given the highest score on the gustatory meaning (Chen et al. 2019), while it would be regarded as a tactile item based on etymological clues. These two methods, however, are not strictly contradictory, as both reveal interesting and complementary linguistic perspectives. That is, the experimental method reveals the synchronic conceptual accessibility of different concepts represented by sensory words in a specific language. Multiple factors can influence this accessibility, such as the frequency of usages and the familiarity of the word for human subjects (Gibbs 2011). In addition, the accessibility of different sensory concepts in sensory items might reflect the contemporary endpoint of diachronic synaesthetic transfers. On the contrary, what can be found from the diachronic approach is the mapping course between senses. The diachronic approach has been used widely in previous research on linguistic synaesthesia. Thus, this study adopted an analogous method to ones used in most reported studies to facilitate a comparison on the tendencies of linguistic synaesthesia in Mandarin Chinese and linguistic synaesthesia in other languages.

2.1.2 Classification of Human Sensory Modalities

Classification of human sensory modalities is also important for the identification of linguistic synaesthesia, as transfer patterns of linguistic synaesthesia differ according to the framework of human senses adopted.

No consensus exists for the definition and classification of the human senses scientifically. For instance, Miller and Johnson-Laird (1976) divided the senses into vision, audition, taste, olfaction, and touch, of which tactile sensations include temperature, pressure, pain, and so forth. Purves et al. (2001 [2000]) proposed a much finer-grained classification for human sensory modalities with more layers than Miller and Johnson-Laird (1976). The study classified human senses into five categories: (1) somatic sensation, which includes perceptions experienced from mechanical stimuli (e.g., light touch, pressure, cutaneous tension, etc.), painful stimuli, and temperature; (2) vision; (3) audition; (4) vestibular sensation; and (5) chemical sensation, which is associated with the nose and mouth. Studies on linguistic synaesthesia such as Williams (1976), Strik Lievers (2015), and Zhao et al. (2018b), however, have widely followed the classification of human senses based on the sensory organs proposed by Aristotle, as the sensory model is intuitive and compatible with linguistic uses (see Miller and Johnson-Laird 1976). It is intriguing that such a sensory organ-based classification of the human senses has also been proposed in Buddhism (see Karunadasa 2014, 2015), which is quite a different philosophy than Aristotelianism. With respect to the sensory classification model based on sensory organs in these two philosophies, there has been little evidence to show an inherited relation. Thus, this study also followed the sensory organ-based classification of human sensory modalities, taking the perceptions experienced by eyes for vision, ears for hearing, the tongue for taste, the nose for smell, and the skin, hands, and muscles for touch. Take Mandarin sensory adjectives for example: 亮 *liang4* 'bright' is a visual adjective, 响 *xiang3* 'loud' is an auditory adjective, 咸 *xian2* 'salty' is a gustatory adjective, 臭 *chou4* 'smelly' is an olfactory adjective, while 软 *ruan3* 'soft', 冷 *leng3* 'cold', and 痛 *tong4* 'painful' are all tactile adjectives.

2.1.3 Data Collection of Synaesthetic Expressions

The following steps were employed to collect synaesthetic examples of Mandarin sensory adjectives from the Sinica corpus.

1. Strik Lievers et al. (2013) and Strik Lievers and Huang (2016) proposed a corpus-based approach for the extraction of linguistic synaesthesia, which includes three steps: compiling perception-related lexical items, searching for sentences containing at least two perception-related items from two different senses, and manually checking the extracted expressions to select the synaesthetic usages. Following this method, this study extracted Mandarin sensory adjectives automatically from two Chinese lexical thesauri, namely, 哈工大信息检索研究中心同义词词林扩展版 HIT-CIR Tongyici Cilin (Extended) (Che et al. 2010) and 知网 HowNet (Dong and Dong 2003).
2. Six lists of Mandarin sensory adjectives were compiled, based on the basic sensory meanings of these adjectives. Five of these word lists are adjectives composed of morphemes with the same etymology in terms of sensory modalities, one list per human sense, including touch, taste, vision, hearing, and

smell. The remaining list contains adjectives consisting of morphemes with different sensory origins.

3. The adjectives in the compiled lists were searched one by one in the Sinica corpus, and were manually checked to determine whether they were used for senses other than their basic sensory modalities. The identification of synaesthetic uses for Mandarin sensory adjectives in this study include two categories:

   (i) For adjectives composed of morphemes with the same sensory origin, the synaesthetic usage of one adjective was noted when the usage was related to a different sensory modality than the adjective's basic sensory domain. For example, the tactile adjective 柔软 *rou2-ruan3* 'soft', consisting of the tactile morphemes 柔 *rou2* 'soft' and 软 *ruan3* 'soft', was considered a synaesthetic use in the expression 柔软的童音 *rou2-ruan3 de tong2-yin1* 'the soft voice of children', since the adjective was employed to describe an auditory perception rather than a tactile perception.[8,9],

   (ii) For adjectives composed of morphemes with different sensory origins, a synaesthetic use was noted when the sensory usage of an adjective differs from both sensory modalities of the adjective's constituent morphemes. For instance, the olfactory use of the adjective 浓烈 *nong2-lie4* 'strong' in the expression 浓烈刺鼻的油漆味 *nong2-lie4 ci4-bi2 de you2-qi1 wei4* 'the strong and pungent smell of paint' was regarded as an instance of linguistic synaesthesia, as the constituent morpheme 浓 *nong2* 'of intense taste' is related to taste, and the morpheme 烈 *lie4* 'scorching' is concerned with temperature in touch, neither of which belong to smell.

Therefore, the linguistic synaesthesia identification procedure (LSIP) designed for extracting Mandarin synaesthetic data can be summarized in following steps, which should be applicable to identifying linguistic synaesthetic instances in other languages:

1) Extracting perception-related items for a specific language;
2) Classifying sensory modalities;
3) Determining the basic sensory domains for the extracted sensory items;
4) Compiling sensory lists based on the basic sensory domains of the extracted sensory items;
5) Extracting usages of the sensory items in the compiled lists from corpora;
6) Manually checking whether the extracted usages of sensory items are related to sensory modalities that are not the basic sensory domains of the items;
7) If yes, marking the usages as instances of linguistic synaesthesia.

---

[8]This study followed the word segmentation in the Sinica corpus to avoid unnecessary dispute; thus, for instance, it treats 柔软 *rou2-ruan3* 'soft' as a compound adjective instead of a phrase containing two monosyllabic adjectives. For more information about word segmentation, please see Chen et al. (1996).

[9]For readability, the part-of-speech tags for collected synaesthetic examples were deleted, and traditional characters were converted into simplified characters.

2.2 Overview of Extracted Data

This section will give an overview for the extracted synaesthetic data of Mandarin sensory adjectives in three aspects: (1) the number of lexical types and tokens identified for each kind of adjectives; (2) the percentage of adjectives with synaesthetic usages among all adjectives in each of five modalities; and (3) the association patterns between different senses in the collected synaesthetic data for Mandarin sensory adjectives.

2.2.1 *Distributions of Synaesthetic Data*

Based on the proposed LSIP, there are 260 Mandarin sensory adjectives with synaesthetic uses in the Sinica corpus, as shown in Table 2.1.

Visual adjectives, tactile adjectives, and compound adjectives composed of morphemes with different sensory origins (i.e., the adjectives grouped in OTHERS in Table 2.1), are the top three lexical types in the extracted synaesthetic data. They have the percentages of occurrence of 38.1% (99/260), 28.1% (73/260), and 23.4% (61/260) respectively.[10] Olfactory and auditory adjectives are much less frequently found with linguistic synaesthesia usages by lexical type, with the respective percentages of 0.8% (2/260) and 1.5% (4/260).

There are 8620 synaesthetic instances of Mandarin adjectives from the Sinica corpus. Among the instances, synaesthetic examples of Mandarin visual and tactile adjectives occupy the two largest proportions with 35.2% (3034/8620) and 31.3% (2695/8620) respectively, as illustrated in Table 2.1.

2.2.2 *Synaesthetic Participation*

Strik Lievers (2015) proposed that lexical differentiation of sensory modalities (i.e., numbers of lexicalized words for a specific sensory modality), especially the richness of adjectives in the vocabulary in a language, could predict the possibility of sensory words used for linguistic synaesthesia. In other words, if one sensory modality has more lexicalized adjectives in the language, sensory words belonging to that sensory modality would be more likely to occur in linguistic synaesthesia, in accordance with Strik Lievers (2015). Winter (2016a) added three factors, including frequency, affective valence, and iconicity of lexical items, to predict whether a

---

[10]The percentage of the adjectives in the OTHERS group was not rounded off to 23.5%, for the sake of the sum of all percentages to be 100%.

Table 2.1 Distributions of synaesthetic data for Mandarin sensory adjectives

	Lexical types		Lexical tokens	
	Number	Percentage (%)	Number	Percentage (%)
VISION	99	**38.1**	3034	**35.2**
TOUCH	73	**28.1**	2695	**31.3**
OTHERS*	61	**23.4**	538	6.2
TASTE	21	8.1	2291	26.6
HEARING	4	1.5	30	0.3
SMELL	2	0.8	32	0.4
TOTAL	260	100	8620	100

*OTHERS = Compound adjectives combining different sensory modalities

sensory item is likely to be used synaesthetically. This study focuses more on how sensory words are used in linguistic synaesthesia than whether sensory words in general are likely to be involved in linguistic synaesthesia. Nevertheless, a brief look at what kinds of Mandarin sensory items tend to have synaesthetic usages (i.e., synaesthetic participation) would facilitate a general understanding of the motivations underlying linguistic synaesthesia.

Table 2.2 shows the synaesthetic participation rates of the compiled Mandarin sensory adjectives with synaesthetic usages (see Sect. 2.1.3). As Table 2.2 indicates, vision has the most lexicalized adjectives in Mandarin (664 lexical types), similar to English (Strik Lievers 2015; Winter 2016a). In addition, visual adjectives are the most likely to have synaesthetic usages in Mandarin, with 99 lexical types. However, the synaesthetic participation rate of visual adjectives (14.9% [99/664]) is much lower than the rates of gustatory (84% [21/25]) and tactile (61.3% [73/119]) adjectives in Mandarin (see Table 2.2). With respect to tactile sensations in Mandarin, both the lexical differentiation of adjectives (i.e., 73 different adjectives in the category) and the synaesthetic participation rate (61.3% [73/119]) are high. Thus, lexical differentiation would not be a good predictor for Mandarin sensory adjectives in terms of their synaesthetic participation, if the percentage of lexical types is taken into account rather than the absolute number.

As demonstrated in Table 2.2, touch and taste are the two sensory modalities with high synaesthetic participation rates (greater than 50%). As suggested by Shen (1997), these two senses, necessarily involving physical contact between sensory organs and perceived objects, are more embodied than the other three modalities (i.e., vision, hearing, and smell), which generally act as source domains in linguistic synaesthesia. With respect to the specific synaesthetic tendencies of these two modalities in Mandarin, Chaps. 3 and 4 will further explore those findings.

Following Winter (2016a), this study also examines the synaesthetic participation rate of the top 10% of the most frequent Mandarin sensory adjectives for each

Table 2.2 Synaesthetic participation rates of Mandarin sensory adjectives for the five senses

	Synaesthetic adjectives (lexical types)	Sensory adjectives (lexical types)[a]	Synaesthetic participation rate
TASTE	21	25	**84%**
TOUCH	**73**	**119**	**61.3%**
HEARING	4	13	30.8%
SMELL	2	10	20%
VISION	**99**	**664**	14.9%

[a]Although the collected sensory adjectives for the five senses in Mandarin cannot be considered exhaustive, they could still provide a general picture of the lexical differentiation for these sensory modalities in the language. As noted by Strik Lievers (2015) and Zhao et al. (2019), the lexical differentiation for the five senses might be related to the characteristics of human perception and cognition. For instance, vision having the most lexicalized adjectives is consistent with the predominance of visual experiences in the human perception system, while smell having the least lexicalized adjectives makes sense when considering the intimacy between tasting and smelling, in which the widespread usage of gustatory adjectives to describe olfactory experiences are grounded (Strik Lievers 2015; Zhao et al. 2019).

sense based on the Sinica corpus. As illustrated in Table 2.3, among these adjectives, over 40% of them have been attested to involve synaesthetic usages, hence supporting Winter's (2016a) prediction that more frequent sensory items are more likely to participate in cross-modal mappings. One exception to the prediction was found in Mandarin auditory adjectives. There is only one adjective among the top 10% of the most frequent auditory adjectives in Mandarin. The adjective is 响 *xiang3* 'loud', which was not found with synaesthetic uses in the Sinica corpus. However, the exception can be explained, as hearing has been demonstrated to rarely occur as a source domain in synaesthetic transfers (see Ullmann 1957; Williams 1976; Zhao and Huang 2018).[11]

Based on the data, one can conclude that lexical differentiation would not be a good predictor for whether a specific Mandarin sensory adjective is likely to be involved in linguistic synaesthesia. Nevertheless, the word frequency of sensory adjectives can function effectively to predict the likelihood of synaesthetic participation for the adjectives in Mandarin.

2.2.3 *Sensory Association*

Studies on the sensory lexicon in languages have shown the interrelation between different sensory modalities. For instance, Lynott and Connell (2009, 2013), Winter (2016a, b, 2019a) demonstrated that there are significant correlations between vision and touch, between taste and smell, and between vision and hearing, based on

[11]The predictors of lexical valence and iconicity for synaesthetic participation proposed by Winter (2016a) cannot be tested by the corpus data in this study; thus, I leave it for future research.

Table 2.3 Synaesthetic participation rates of the top 10% of the most frequent Mandarin sensory adjectives for the five senses

	Synaesthetic adjectives (lexical types)	Sensory adjectives (lexical types)	Synaesthetic participation rate
TASTE	3	2.5 (≈ 3)	100%
SMELL	1	1	100%
TOUCH	10	11.9 (≈ 12)	83.3%
VISION	29	66.4 (≈ 66)	43.9%
HEARING	0	1.3 (≈ 1)	0

statistical analyses of perceptual ratings on English sensory words. Chen et al. (2019) confirmed these connections between the five senses in Mandarin sensory adjectives. However, these studies did not take into consideration the directionality of these associations between the senses. On the contrary, not only the interrelations, but also the directional patterns of associations between the senses can be observed in Mandarin synaesthetic adjectives identified in the Sinica corpus.

Table 2.4 shows that Mandarin tactile adjectives are the most likely to be used for vision, with the probability of 84.9% (62/73) in terms of lexical types. This tendency is consistent with the observation of the significant correlation between touch and vision by previous experimental studies (Lynott and Connell 2009, 2013; Chen et al. 2019). Such an association between touch and vision, however, is not bi-directional, as visual adjectives for touch are not as productive as tactile adjectives for vision, as illustrated in Table 2.4.

The association between taste and smell among Mandarin synaesthetic adjectives is similar to that between touch and vision. Specifically speaking, gustatory adjectives are most likely to be associated with smell, and olfactory adjectives are most likely to be associated with taste in Mandarin. Specifically, gustatory adjectives for smell are more frequent than olfactory adjectives for taste, with the probabilities of 76.2% (16/21) and 50% (1/2) by lexical type respectively (see Table 2.4).

Table 2.4 Sensory associations in Mandarin synaesthetic adjectives

Source domains	Target domains					Total
	TOUCH	TASTE	VISION	HEARING	SMELL	
TOUCH	–	7	**62**	41	15	73
	–	9.6%	**84.9%**	56.2%	20.5%	–
TASTE	5	–	12	11	**16**	21
	23.8%	–	57.1%	52.4%	**76.2%**	–
VISION	18	10	–	**87**	13	99
	18.2%	10.1%	–	**87.9%**	13.1%	–
HEARING	0	0	**4**	–	0	4
	0	0	**100%**	–	0	–
SMELL	0	**1**	**1**	0	–	2
	0	**50%**	**50%**	0	–	–
Total	23	18	79	139	44	–

It is remarkable that the association between vision and hearing in Mandarin synaesthetic adjectives is different from those between touch and vision and between taste and smell. That is, the probability of visual adjectives for hearing (87.9% [87/99] is close to that of auditory adjectives for vision (100% [4/4]) in Mandarin synaesthetic adjectives, as shown in Table 2.4.

The ratios of synaesthetic sources to synaesthetic targets for each sensory modality can also be calculated with respect to lexical type, from the largest to the smallest: TOUCH (3.17 [73/23]) > VISION (1.25 [99/79]) > TASTE (1.17 [21/18]) > SMELL (0.05 [2/44]) > HEARING (0.03 [4/139]). The ratio rank can be regarded as an indication that touch, taste, and vision are more likely to be sources in sensory associations, while smell and hearing are more likely to be targets.[12]

Hence, significant associations between the five senses found in experimental studies also appear in the empirical data from the corpus, including the associations between touch and vision, between taste and smell, and between vision and hearing. Moreover, the corpus data could also imply that most of the associations between senses tend to follow directional tendencies. Chapters 3 through 6 will examine the directional tendencies of sensory associations for Mandarin synaesthetic adjectives in depth.

2.3 Summary of the Chapter

This chapter has proposed a linguistic synaesthesia identification procedure (LSIP) and presented an overview of the extracted data for Mandarin synaesthetic adjectives. In order to elaborate on LSIP, I discussed the identification process for the basic sensory meanings for Mandarin sensory adjectives, the classification of human senses, and steps for extraction of the synaesthetic uses of Mandarin sensory adjectives from the Sinica corpus. In addition, LSIP could also be applicable to the identification of linguistic synaesthesia in other languages, based on the specific steps of LSIP summarized.

The overview of the extracted synaesthetic data has shown that visual adjectives and tactile adjectives are the most involved in linguistic synaesthesia, with respect to both lexical types and lexical tokens. However, tactile and gustatory adjectives have been demonstrated to exhibit much higher synaesthetic participation rates than visual, auditory, and olfactory adjectives in Mandarin. In addition, the overview has

[12]One should acknowledge that there might be a risk in generalizing the tendencies of Mandarin synaesthesia based on the limited numbers of auditory and olfactory adjectives collected (i.e., four and two respectively). Nevertheless, the limited lexical types for hearing and smell are likely to result from the characteristics of human cognition (see Footnote in Table 2.2). In addition, in terms of a corpus-based study, word types and word tokens are generally considered in research on linguistic synaesthesia, such as Strik Lievers (2015) and Zhao et al. (2018b). Therefore, this book leaves how to interpret the limited data for the synaesthetic tendencies of auditory and olfactory modalities in Mandarin more appropriately for future studies.

also demonstrated that the associations between touch and vision, between taste and smell, and between vision and hearing reported by experimental studies can be attested in the collected corpus data. Apart from confirming the relationship between the five senses, the corpus data can also indicate that the associations between senses are likely not random, but instead exhibit directional tendencies.

The following chapters will explore the directional tendencies of sensory associations reflected in linguistic synaesthetic expressions for Mandarin Chinese in detail. As Mandarin tactile adjectives are productive in synaesthetic usages, in terms of adjective types, token examples, and synaesthetic participation rates (see Sect. 2.2), the next chapter will focus on the transfer tendencies and underlying mechanisms of linguistic synaesthesia for Mandarin tactile adjectives first.

References

Biber, Douglas E. 2012. Corpus-based and corpus-driven analyses of language variation and use. In *The oxford handbook of linguistic analysis*, ed. Bernd Heine and Heiko Narrog, 159–192. Oxford: Oxford University Press.

Burgers, Christian, Margot Van Mulken, and Peter Jan Schellens. 2011. Finding irony: An introduction of the verbal irony procedure (VIP). *Metaphor and Symbol* 26(3): 186–205.

Che, Wanxiang, Zhenghua Li and Ting Liu. 2010. LTP: A Chinese language technology platform. In *Proceedings of the 23rd international conference on computational linguistics: Demonstrations*, 13–16.

Chen, Keh-Jiann, Chu-Ren Huang, Li-Ping Chang and Hui-Li Hsu. 1996. Sinica corpus: Design methodology for balanced corpora. In *Proceedings of the 11th Pacific Asia conference on language, information and computation (PACLIC 11)*, 167–176.

Chen, I-Hsuan, Qingqing Zhao, Yunfei Long, Qin Lu, and Chu-Ren Huang. 2019. Mandarin Chinese modality exclusivity norms. *PLoS ONE* 14(2): e0211336.

Chou, Ya-Min, and Chu-Ren Huang. 2010. Hantology: Conceptual system discovery based on orthographic convention. In *Ontology and the lexicon: A natural language processing perspective*, ed. Chu-Ren Huang, Nicoletta Calzolari, Aldo Gangemi, Alessandro Lenci, Alessandro Oltramari, and Laurent Prévot, 122–143. Cambridge: Cambridge University Press.

D.C. Lau Research Centre. 2005. *Chinese ancient texts database (CHANT)*. Hong Kong: Institute of Chinese Studies (ICS) of the Chinese University of Hong Kong.

Dong, Zhengdong and Qiang Dong. 2003. HowNet—A hybrid language and knowledge resource. In *Proceedings of natural language processing and knowledge engineering*, 820–824.

Duan, Yucai (段玉裁). 2007 [1735–1815]. *Commentary on explaining graphs and analyzing characters* [说文解字注]. Nanjing [南京]: Phoenix Press [凤凰出版社].

Gibbs, Raymond W. 2011. Evaluating conceptual metaphor theory. *Discourse Processes* 48(8): 529–562.

Huang, Chu-Ren, and Shu-Kai Hsieh. 2015. Chinese lexical semantics: From radicals to event structure. In *The Oxford handbook of Chinese linguistics*, ed. William S.-Y. Wang and Chao-Fen Sun, 290–305. New York: Oxford University Press.

Huang, Chu-Ren, and Jiajuan Xiong. 2019. Linguistic synaesthesia in Chinese. In *The Routledge handbook of applied Chinese linguistics*, ed. Chu-Ren Huang, Zhuo Jing-Schmidt, and Barbara Meisterernst, 294–312. London: Routledge.

Karunadasa, Yakupitiyage. 2014. *The Theravāda Abhidhamma: Its inquiry into the nature of conditioned reality*. Hong Kong: The University of Hong Kong.

Karunadasa, Yakupitiyage. 2015. *The Buddhist analysis of matter*. Hong Kong: The University of Hong Kong.

Lehrer, Adrienne. 1978. Structures of the lexicon and transfer of meaning. *Lingua* 45(2): 95–123.

Lievers, Francesca Strik. 2015. Synaesthesia: A corpus-based study of cross-modal directionality. *Functions of Language* 22(1): 69–95.

Lynott, Dermot, and Louise Connell. 2009. Modality exclusivity norms for 423 object properties. *Behavior Research Methods* 41(2): 558–564.

Lynott, Dermot, and Louise Connell. 2013. Modality exclusivity norms for 400 nouns: The relationship between perceptual experience and surface word form. *Behavior Research Methods* 45(2): 516–526.

Meyer, Charles F. 2014. Corpus-based and corpus-driven approaches to linguistic analysis: One and the samhie? In *Developments in English: Expanding Electronic Evidence (Studies in English Language)*, ed. Irma Taavitsainen, Merja Kytö, Claudia Claridge, Jeremy Smith, and Fukka Tuominen, 14–28. Cambridge: Cambridge University Press.

Miller, George, and Philip Johnson-Laird. 1976. *Language and perception*. Cambridge, London and Melbourne: Cambridge University Press.

Pragglejaz Group. 2007. MIP: A method for identifying metaphorically used words in discourse. *Metaphor and Symbol* 22(1): 1–39.

Purves, Dale, George J. Augustine, David Fitzpatrick, Lawrence C. Katz, Anthony-Samuel LaMantia, James O. McNamara and S. Mark Williams (eds.). 2001 [2000]. *Neuroscience* (2nd ed.). Massachusetts: Sinauer Associates, Inc.

Semino, Elena. 2010. Descriptions of pain, metaphor, and embodied simulation. *Metaphor and Symbol* 25(4): 205–226.

Shen, Yeshayahu. 1997. Cognitive constraints on poetic figures. *Cognitive Linguistics* 8(1): 33–71.

Steen, Gerard. 1999. From linguistic to conceptual metaphor in five steps. In *Metaphor in cognitive linguistics: Selected papers from the 5th international cognitive linguistics conference*, ed. Raymond W. Gibbs and Gerard J. Steen, 57–77. Amsterdam and Philadelphia: John Benjamins Publishing Company.

Steen, Gerard, Aletta Dorst, Berenike Herrmann, Anna Kaal, Tina Krennmayr, and Trijntje Pasma. 2010. *A method for linguistic metaphor identification: From MIP to MIPVU*. Amsterdam and Philadelphia: John Benjamins Publishing Company.

Strik Lievers, Francesca, Ge Xu and Hongzhi Xu. 2013. A methodology for the extraction of lexicalized synaesthesia from corpora. Paper presented at *The 19th international congress of linguists*. Université de Genève, 21–27 July.

Strik Lievers, Francesca and Chu-Ren Huang. 2016. A lexicon of perception for the identification of synaesthetic metaphors in corpora. In *Proceedings of the 10th language resources and evaluation conference (LREC 2016)*, 4032–4036.

Ullmann, Stephen. 1957. *The principles of semantics*. Oxford: Basil Blackwell.

Wang, Ning (王宁). 1996. *The principle in etymological studies on Chinese* [训诂学原理]. Beijing [北京]: China International Radio Press [中国国际广播出版社].

Williams, Joseph. 1976. Synaesthetic adjectives: A possible law of sematic change. *Language* 52 (2): 461–478.

Winter, Bodo. 2016a. *The sensory structure of the English lexicon*. Merced, CA: University of California, Merced dissertation.

Winter, Bodo. 2016b. Taste and smell words form an affectively loaded and emotionally flexible part of the English lexicon. *Language, Cognition and Neuroscience* 31(8): 975–988.

Winter, Bodo. 2019a. *Sensory linguistics: Language, perception and metaphor*. Amsterdam and Philadelphia: John Benjamins Publishing Company.

Xu, Shen (许慎). 1963 [156]. *Explaining graphs and analyzing characters* [说文解字]. Beijing [北京]: Zhonghua Book Company [中华书局].

Xu, Zhongshu (徐中舒). 2010 [1986]. *Great compendium of Chinese characters* [汉语大字典] (2nd ed.). Chengdu [成都] and Wuhan [武汉]: Sichuan Dictionary Publishing Company [四川辞书出版社] and Hubei Dictionary Publishing Company [湖北辞书出版社].

Yu, Ning. 2003. Synesthetic metaphors: A cognitive perspective. *Journal of Literary Semantics* 32 (1): 19–34.

Zhao, Qingqing (赵青青) and Chu-Ren Huang (黄居仁). 2018. Mapping models and underlying mechanisms of synaesthetic metaphors in Mandarin [现代汉语通感隐喻的映射模型与制约机制]. *Language Teaching and Linguistic Studies* [语言教学与研究] 1: 44–55.

Zhao, Qingqing, Chu-Ren Huang, and Yunfei Long. 2018b. Synaesthesia in Chinese: A corpus-based study on gustatory adjectives in Mandarin. *Linguistics* 56(5): 1167–1194.

Zhao, Qingqing (赵青青), Jiajuan Xiong (熊佳娟) and Chu-Ren Huang (黄居仁). 2019. Linguistic synaesthesia, metaphor, and cognition: The systematicity and significance of linguistic synaesthesia in Chinese [通感、隐喻与认知—通感现象在汉语中的系统性表现与语言学价值]. *Zhuoguoyuwen* [中国语文] 2: 240–253.

Chapter 3
Mandarin Tactile Adjectives

Shen (1997) and Popova (2005) have both suggested that touch is the most embodied sensory modality among human senses based on its perceptual nature. That is, touch necessarily involves physical contact between sensory organs and perceived objects, generally produces affective contents, and is able to be experienced through multiple sensory organs (e.g., hands, skins, and muscles) (Shen 1997; Popova 2005). Following this, one could predict that tactile words in the language could be involved in synaesthetic uses for the other four senses.

The biological association account of linguistic synaesthesia does not provide any explicit prediction on the directionality of synaesthetic transfers between sensory modalities. However, the theory has demonstrated crucial physiological connections between different perceptions to account for linguistic synaesthesia. These include the association between sharp taste (taste) and high temperature (touch) in pungency (Hirasa and Takemasa 1998; Zhao et al. 2018), the neural connection between spicy taste (taste) and pain (touch) (Caterina et al. 1997; Rakova 2003), and the co-activation of touch and vision in perceiving shapes (Amedi et al. 2002).

This chapter will determine the transfer tendencies of linguistic synaesthesia for Mandarin tactile adjectives, based on the distribution of the synaesthetic uses of these adjectives in the Sinica corpus. In addition, it will examine the explanatory power of the different theoretical accounts for linguistic synaesthesia in Mandarin tactile adjectives. Specifically, Sect. 3.1 will present the data distribution for the synaesthetic usages of Mandarin tactile adjectives; Sect. 3.2 will be concentrated on Mandarin adjectives for tactile intensity, and Sect. 3.3 will focus on Mandarin adjectives for specific tactile perceptions. The last section is a summary of the synaesthetic tendencies of Mandarin tactile adjectives.

Q. Zhao, *Embodied Conceptualization or Neural Realization*,
Frontiers in Chinese Linguistics 10, https://doi.org/10.1007/978-981-32-9315-1_3

Table 3.1 Sub-types of touch for Mandarin tactile synaesthetic adjectives

Tactile sub-types		Numbers of adjectives	Examples of adjectives
Intensity		3	强 *qiang2* 'strong' 弱 *ruo4* 'weak'
Quality	Temperature	21	冷 *leng3* 'cold' 暖 *nuan3* 'warm'
	Hardness	16	软 *ruan3* 'soft' 硬 *ying4* 'hard
	Sharpness	9	钝 *dun4* 'blunt' 锋利 *feng1-li4* 'sharp'
	Dampness	7	湿 *shi1* 'wet' 干燥 *gan1-zao4* 'dry'
	Smoothness	7	滑 *hua2* 'smooth' 粗糙 *cu1-cao1* 'rough'
	Physical force	6	重 *zhong4* 'heavy' 轻 *qing1* 'light (in weight)'
	Pain	4	麻 *ma2* 'trembling' 刺 *ci4* 'stabbing'

3.1 Data Distributions

There are 73 Mandarin tactile adjectives with synaesthetic uses identified in the Sinica corpus, of which 2695 token examples were extracted (cf. Table 2.1 in Chap. 2).

Most of these adjectives conceptualize specific tactile perceptions including temperature, hardness, sharpness, and so forth (e.g., 冷 *leng3* 'cold', 硬 *ying4* 'hard', and 锋利 *feng1-li4* 'sharp'), based on the ontological categories in 哈工大信息检索研究中心同义词词林扩展版 HIT-CIR Tongyici Cilin (Extended) and 知网 HowNet. There are only three adjectives denoting tactile intensity rather than the specific tactile quality, such as 强 *qiang2* 'strong' and 弱 *ruo4* 'weak', as shown in Table 3.1. These Mandarin adjectives for different sub-types of touch will be discussed separately one by one, given their different transfer patterns and interpretations in linguistic synaesthesia. A more detailed data summary of the distribution of synaesthetic uses for each tactile adjective can be found in Appendix A.

3.2 Tactile Adjectives of Intensity

The three Mandarin synaesthetic adjectives for tactile intensity were found to have distributions in taste, vision, hearing, and smell in the Sinica corpus, as predicted by the embodiment account. Specifically, one of them, 强烈 *qiang2-lie4* 'strong', characterizes the intensity of gustatory perceptions, as illustrated in example (1).

(1) Tactile adjectives of intensity used for taste

伏特加 *fu2-te4-jia1*	的 *de*	**强烈 *qiang2-lie4***[TOUCH/SOURCE]
vodka	GEN	strong-scorching
味道 *wei4-dao*[TASTE/TARGET]		穿过 *chuan1-guo4*
flavor-path		pass-through
喉头 *hou2-tou2*		
throat-head		

'The intense taste of vodka passes through the throat.'

All three tactile intensity adjectives have distributions in vision. Following Williams (1976: 476), adjectives originally for visual color/light (termed as "color") and adjectives for dimension/shape (termed as "dimension") were distinguished from other visual types, which were named as "visual situation" collectively for discussion in this study. For instance, a beautiful appearance, a secluded surrounding, a dense arrangement of objects, and so on, cannot be included in either color or dimension. Thus, I name all these things as visual situation, which are generally perceived visually but neither color/light nor dimension/shape.

Examples (2) and (3) show that the three tactile intensity adjectives can all be used for color and visual situation for perceptual intensity, while none exhibits synaesthetic uses for visual dimension.

(2) Tactile adjectives of intensity used for color (vision)

a. **光线 *guang1-xian4***[VISION/TARGET]

light-line

越來越 *yue4-lai2-yue4*	**强 *qiang2***[TOUCH/SOURCE]
increasingly-ASP-increasingly	strong

'The light becomes stronger and stronger.'

b. **<u>用色 *yong4-se4*</u>**[VISION/TARGET] **<u>强烈 *qiang2-lie4*</u>**[TOUCH/SOURCE]

use-color strong-scorching

鲜艳 *xian1-yan4*

tasty-colorful

'The color used is strong and bright.'

c. 幽幽 *you1-you1* 的 *de* **<u>弱 *ruo4*</u>**[TOUCH/SOURCE]

faint-faint NOM weak

<u>光 *guang1*</u>[VISION/TARGET]

light

'the faint and weak light'

(3) Tactile adjectives of intensity used for visual situation (vision)

a. **<u>线条感 *xian4-tiao2-gan3*</u>**[VISION/TARGET] **<u>强 *qiang2*</u>**[TOUCH/SOURCE]

line-line-perception strong

'the visual perception of lines is strong.'

b. **<u>强烈 *qiang2-lie4*</u>**[TOUCH/SOURCE] 而 *er2* 深刻 *shen1-ke4*

strong-scorching and deep-carving

的 *de* **<u>视觉 *shi4-jue2* 影像 *ying3-xiang4*</u>**[VISION/TARGET]

NOM vision-sense image-image

'the strong and impressive visual image'

c. <u>**眼 *yan3* 中 *zhong1* 的 *de***</u>

eye center GEN

<u>**电芒 *dian4-mang2***</u>[VISION/TARGET] 逐渐 *zhu2-jian4*

electricity-light gradually-gradually

减 *jian3* <u>**弱 *ruo4***</u>[TOUCH/SOURCE]

reduce weak

'The gleam in the eyes becomes weak gradually.'

These three tactile intensity adjectives also have distributions in hearing for auditory intensity, as illustrated in example (4).

(4) Tactile adjectives of intensity used for hearing

a. <u>**鼾声 *han1-sheng1***</u>[HEARING/TARGET] [...]

snore-sound [...]

渐 *jian4* <u>**强 *qiang2***</u>[TOUCH/SOURCE]

gradually strong

'The sound of snoring becomes strong gradually.'

b. <u>**强烈 *qiang2-lie4***</u> [TOUCH/SOURCE] 的 *de*

strong-scorching NOM

<u>**节奏 *jie2-zou4***</u>[HEARING/TARGET]

rhythm-rhythm

'the strong rhythm'

c. 她 *ta1* **<u>听 *ting1*</u>**[HEARING/TARGET] 瓦耳拉齐 *wa3-er3-la1-qi2*

she listen Waerlaqi

的 *de* **<u>气息 *qi4-xi1*</u>**[HEARING/TARGET] 渐 *jian4*

GEN air-breath gradually

<u>弱 *ruo4*</u>[TOUCH/SOURCE]

weak

'She heard the breath of Waerlaqi becoming weak gradually.'

There is only one tactile intensity adjective with synaesthetic distributions in the olfactory domain, i.e., 强烈 *qiang2-lie4* 'strong', characterizing the strong perceptual intensity of smell, as shown in example (5).

(5) Tactile adjectives of intensity used for smell

一股 *yi1-gu3* **<u>强烈 *qiang2-lie4*</u>**[TOUCH/SOURCE] 的 *de*

one-CL strong-scorching NOM

<u>香味 *xiang1-wei4*</u>[SMELL/TARGET]

fragrant-flavor

'a strong fragrance'

The synaesthetic uses of Mandarin tactile intensity adjectives are thus consistent with the prediction of the embodiment account of linguistic synaesthesia, where distributions of the tactile adjectives in taste, vision, hearing, and smell were all attested. In terms of the interpretation of these intensity adjectives in linguistic synaesthesia, the perceived similarity of perceptual intensity is also suggested to ground associations in different sensory modalities proposed by the embodiment account. Specifically, extensive studies have found that adjectives encode not only specific concepts but also scalar polarity inherently in their lexical semantics, such as Lehrer and Lehrer (1982), Lehrer (1985), Kennedy (1999), Kennedy and McNally (2005), Kennedy and McNally (2009), and so on. With respect to Mandarin tactile intensity adjectives, they not only preserve their intensity concepts, but also retain the scalar polarity when used for linguistic synaesthesia. For instance, 强 *qiang2* 'strong' and 强烈 *qiang2-lie4* 'strong', originally conceptualizing the positive pole of the intensity scale, were still used to characterize the strong intensity perceived by the gustatory sense illustrated in (1), by the visual sense in (2a), (2b), (3a), and (3b), by the auditory sense in (4a) and (4b), and by the olfactory sense in (5). Similarly, the adjective 弱 *ruo4* 'weak', originally on the negative pole of the tactile intensity scale, was used to denote the weakness of visual and auditory perceptions, as in (2c), (3c), and (4c).

It is interesting to note that among the Mandarin tactile adjectives of intensity, none was found to have synaesthetic uses for dimension in the visual modality. I will return to the issue after determining the general tendency of Mandarin tactile adjectives in linguistic synaesthesia.

3.3 Tactile Adjectives of Quality

The synaesthetic distribution of Mandarin tactile quality adjectives also supports the prediction of the embodiment account of linguistic synaesthesia mapping from the more embodied to the less embodied, as synaesthetic transfers from touch to taste, from touch to vision, from touch to hearing, and from touch to smell were all found in the Sinica corpus. Nevertheless, the theory does not make a prediction for that Mandarin adjectives in different tactile sub-types differ in their transfer patterns (especially the mappings to different visual sub-domains) and in their interpretations when used in linguistic synaesthetic expressions. The following content will be concentrated on the insufficiency of the embodiment account's explanations for linguistic synaesthesia, by demonstrating the specific transfer tendencies and interpretations of Mandarin tactile adjectives for temperature, hardness, sharpness, dampness, smoothness, physical force, and pain.

3.3.1 Temperature

Mandarin tactile adjectives for temperature are most frequently employed in linguistic synaesthesia in terms of the lexical types (i.e., with 21 adjectives), as shown in Table 3.1.

Only one of the adjectives have distributions in taste. The adjective 烈 *lie4* 'scorching' was used to characterize wine with a strong taste, as shown in (6). The perceived similarity of intensity between the high temperature of fire and the strong taste of wine could be regarded as an underlying basis for the sensory association between touch and taste, as suggested by the embodiment account. Nevertheless, the gustatory use of the adjective 烈 *lie4* 'scorching' is related to the perceptual intensity of gustation rather than a specific taste comparable with sweetness, bitterness, and so forth. Thus, the adjective 烈 *lie4* 'scorching' does not retain the concept of quality represented in touch when used for taste.

(6) Tactile adjectives of temperature used for taste

又 *you4*	香 *xiang1*	又 *you4*	**烈 *lie4***[TOUCH/SOURCE]
additionally	fragrant	additionally	scorching
的 *de*	美 *mei3*	**酒 *jiu4***[TASTE/TARGET]	
NOM	tasty	wine	

'the fragrant, strong, and tasty wine'

There are 20 Mandarin temperature adjectives found to have distributions in vision, of which ten adjectives were used to characterize color and 17 adjectives were employed to describe visual situation, while none was attested to have synaesthetic uses for visual dimension.

The ten Mandarin temperature adjectives with synaesthetic uses for color are 寒 *han2* 'chilling', 冷 *leng3* 'cold', 冰冷 *bing1-leng3* 'ice-cold', 凉 *liang2* 'cool', and 刺冽 *ci4-lie4* 'chilling' for lower temperature, and 暖 *nuan3* 'warm', 温暖 *wen1-nuan3* 'warm', 灼灼 *zhuo2-zhuo2* 'scorching', 炽烈 *chi4-lie4* 'scorching', and 热 *re4* 'hot' for higher temperature. Based on the color theory, colors related to sunlight and fire, such as red and yellow, are warm, while colors related to ice and water, such as blue and green, tend to be cold (see Wyszecki and Stiles 1967). It is intriguing that the linguistic conceptualization of color perceptions in Mandarin Chinese is in line with the perceptual fact observed in the color theory (see Wyszecki and Stiles 1967). As demonstrated in examples (7a) and (7b), the temperature adjective 暖 *nuan3* 'warm' was used to describe a yellow color, and the adjective 凉 *liang2* 'cool' was employed to characterize grayish blue. The correspondence between linguistic patterns and perceptual patterns would thus indicate a sensory integration basis for linguistic synaesthesia. That is, the recurrent associations between color and temperature sensations in specific objects, such as the yellow color and the warm sensation of sunlight and the green color and the cool sensation of water, likely motivate the linguistic conceptualization of color in terms of temperature concepts.[1,2] By contrast, the perceived similarity assumed by the embodiment account would be less obvious in the interpretations of synaesthetic

[1]It makes sense that the conceptualization of color sensations using temperature concepts has been realized in the language, but not the other way around, if the different degrees of embodiment for touch and vision are taken into consideration. That is, the conceptualization of color in terms of temperature is consistent with the cognitive principle of mapping from the more embodied (i.e., touch) to the less embodied (i.e., vision).

[2]Paradis and Eeg-Olofsson (2013: 38) described this kind of linguistic conceptualizations as "synesthetic metonymization". This study does not follow the term, as the term does not capture the nature of the linguistic usages, but instead adds unnecessary confusion to the alternative term of linguistic synaesthesia (i.e., "synaesthetic metaphor"). Thus, these linguistic expressions, whose

uses of Mandarin temperature adjectives for color, as neither the correspondence concerning perceptual intensity or affective evaluation between temperature sensations and color sensations could be established for these adjectives when employed for color.

(7) Tactile adjectives of temperature used for color (vision)[3]

a. **暖 *nuan3***[TOUCH/SOURCE] **黄 *huang2***[VISION/TARGET]

warm yellow

'the warm yellow'

b. 薄 *bao2* **凉 *liang2***[TOUCH/SOURCE] 的 *de*

thin cool NOM

灰蓝色 *hui1-lan2-se4*[VISION/TARGET]

grey-blue-color

'the thin and cool grayish blue'

Mandarin temperature adjectives with synaesthetic uses for visual situation, however, do show the perceived similarity basis for linguistic synaesthesia, as predicted by the embodiment account. That is, adjectives conceptualizing higher, more pleasant temperatures were generally used to denote positive visual sensations, such as (8a) smiling, while adjectives conceptualizing lower, more unpleasant temperatures were employed to characterize negative visual sensations, such as (8b) sneering. This tendency was also found for nine Mandarin temperature adjectives used for hearing, as illustrated in (9), where 温暖 *wen1-nuan3* was used to describe

---

most remarkable characteristic is their being evidence for a sensory integration basis for synaesthetic transfers, are not given a specialized linguistic label in this research.

[3]The color usage of the adjective 凉 *liang2* 'cool' is much less frequent than that of the adjective 暖 *nuan3* 'warm' in the Sinica corpus (i.e., with one and 22 instances respectively), which thus roughly correspond to creative and conventional types of linguistic synaesthesia. As the Sinica corpus contains both fictional and non-fictional texts (Chen et al. 1996), this study does not differentiate the types of linguistic synaesthesia with respect to the degree of conventionalization. Nevertheless, it would be an interesting topic to explore whether there are differences in transfer tendencies and underlying mechanisms between the two types of linguistic synaesthesia in future studies.

a pleasant auditory feeling, while 冰冷 *bing1-leng3* 'ice-cold' was employed to modify the angry voice.

(8) Tactile adjectives of temperature used for visual situation (vision)

a. **<u>温暖 *wen1-nuan3*</u>**[TOUCH/SOURCE] 的 *de*

lukewarm-warm NOM

<u>笑容 *xiao4-rong2*</u>[VISION/TARGET]

smile-appearance

'the warm smile'

b. 一丝 *yi1-si1* **<u>冷 *leng3*</u>**[TOUCH/SOURCE] **<u>笑 *xiao4*</u>**[VISION/TARGET]

one-CL cold smile

'a hint of the cold smile'

(9) Tactile adjectives of temperature used for hearing

a. **<u>温暖 *wen1-nuan3*</u>**[TOUCH/SOURCE] 的 *de*

lukewarm-warm NOM

<u>歌声 *ge1-sheng1*</u>[HEARING/TARGET]

song-sound

'the warm song'

b. **<u>冰冷 *bing1-leng3*</u>**[TOUCH/SOURCE] 愤怒 *fen4-nu4* 的 *de*

ice-cold angry-angry NOM

<u>声音 *sheng1-yin1*</u>[HEARING/TARGET]

sound-voice

'the ice-cold and angry voice'

The synaesthetic transfers from touch to smell appear in four Mandarin tactile adjectives of temperature. The adjectives are 温暖 *wen1-nuan3* 'warm', 热 *re4* 'hot', and 炽热 *chi4-re4* 'scorching' conceptualizing higher temperature, and 冷 *leng3* 'cold' denoting lower temperature.

It is intriguing that, for the olfactory uses of Mandarin temperature adjectives, the correspondence between temperature and smell is difficult to determine, with respect to both perceptual intensity and affective evaluation. For instance, both 冷 *leng3* 'cold' (on the lower part of the temperature scale) and 热 *re4* 'hot' (on the higher part of the temperature scale) were found with synaesthetic uses for the positive olfactory perception, i.e., 香 *xiang1* 'fragrance', in the Sinica corpus.

A closer look at the contextual information, however, could provide suggestive clues. This study has found that all synaesthetic expressions of Mandarin temperature adjectives for smell co-occur with temperature-related items in context, where the temperature-related items encode temperature information congruent with the synaesthetic adjectives in question. For example, the olfactory use of 温暖 *wen1-nuan3* 'warm' was attested to co-occur with 烈日 *lie4-ri4* 'the scorching sun' implying high temperature, as shown in (10a), while the olfactory use of 冷 *leng3* 'cold' was found to have the co-occurrence with 冬*dong1* 'winter' generally concerned with low temperature, as illustrated in (10b). Thus, the distributional pattern of Mandarin temperature adjectives used for smell suggest that linguistic synaesthesia not only can be grounded in perceived similarity, but also can be motivated by sensory integration perceptually, which has been demonstrated by various neural and psychological studies (e.g., Marks 1978; Amedi et al. 2002; Spence 2011; Winter 2016a; among many others). In other words, the olfactory uses of Mandarin temperature adjectives, accompanied by the conceptualization of the congruent temperature perceptions in context, could be considered linguistic realizations of sensory integrations caused by perceptual "spatiotemporal congruency" (Spence 2011: 971). As further evidence will show, there are many other synaesthetic uses of Mandarin sensory adjectives indicating the sensory integration basis for linguistic synaesthesia over the perceived similarity basis or the biological association basis.

(10) Tactile adjectives of temperature used for smell

a.

那 *na4*	腐臭 *fu3-chou4*	发酵 *fa1-jiao4*	的 *de*
that	rotten-smelly	get-fermented	NOM
<u>温暖 *wen1-nuan3*</u>[TOUCH/SOURCE]，			一股 *yi1-gu3*
lukewarm-warm			one-CL
烈日 *lie4-ri4*	下 *xia4*	的 *de*	肥油 *fei2-you2*
scorching-sun	below	NOM	fat-oil
<u>气味 *qi4-wei4*</u>[SMELL/TARGET]			
air-flavor			

'the rotten, smelly, fermented, and warm odor, which is an odor of fat oil in the scorching sun'

(the co-occurring temperature-related item is: 烈日 *lie4-ri4* 'the scorching sun')

b.

入冬 *ru4-dong1*	后 *hou4*	该 *gai1*	像 *xiang4*
enter-winter	after	should	like
温哥华 *wen1-ge1-hua2*	那样 *na4-yang4*		散发 *san4-fa1*
Vancouver	that-sample		emit-emit
着 *zhe1*	一地 *yi1-di4*	的 *de*	银光 *yin2-guang1*
ASP	one-land	NOM	silver-light
与 *yu3*	**<u>冷 *leng3*</u>**[TOUCH/SOURCE]		**<u>香 *xiang1*</u>**[SMELL/TARGET]
and	cold		fragrance

'There should be massive silver light and cold fragrance after winter comes just as in Vancouver.'

(the co-occurring temperature-related item is: 冬 *dong1* 'winter')

3.3.2 Hardness

Mandarin adjectives for tactile hardness were distributed in vision, hearing, and smell, but not in taste.

There are 12 tactile hardness adjectives identified with synaesthetic usages for vision in the Sinica corpus, of which three were employed to describe color, i.e., 柔 *rou2* 'soft', 柔软 *rou2-ruan3* 'soft', and 轻柔 *qing1-rou2* 'soft'. It should be noted that these adjectives were utilized not only for warm colors, such as yellow in (11a), but also for cold colors, such as green in (11b), which is different from the color usages of Mandarin temperature adjectives discussed above. In addition, the interpretations of synaesthetic expressions of the three tactile adjectives for color support the perceived similarity basis for synaesthetic transfers, as their synaesthetic usages generally imply color with pleasant properties. Thus, the synaesthetic pattern is consistent in that the tactile hardness sensations conceptualized by these three adjectives are also generally positive (see Winter 2016a).

(11) Tactile adjectives of hardness used for color (vision)

a. **柔 *rou2***[TOUCH/SOURCE] **黄 *huang2***[VISION/TARGET]

soft yellow

'the soft yellow'

b. **柔 *rou2***[TOUCH/SOURCE] **绿 *lv4***[VISION/TARGET]

soft green

'the soft green'

One interesting pattern emerges from Mandarin adjectives of tactile hardness: There is one adjective (i.e., 烂 *lan4* 'tender') with synaesthetic uses for visual dimension. The distribution has not been attested among Mandarin tactile intensity adjectives or among Mandarin temperature adjectives. As shown in (12), the synaesthetic expression of the adjective 烂 *lan4* 'tender' for dimension conceptualizes the visual fragmented property of physical objects on the surface. This usage is in line with the neural finding that there is a specialized cortical region (i.e., LOtv) in the brain associating touch and vision with a response preference on graspable visual objects for shape perceptions (Amedi et al. 2002). Therefore, one could expect that tactile perceptions experienced typically by grasping (such as hardness, but not temperature) are easier to associate with the visual perception of dimension physiologically than other tactile perceptions. Mandarin adjectives of tactile hardness (but not adjectives of temperature) with synaesthetic uses for visual dimension would thus be the linguistic realization of the neural association.

Therefore, the synaesthetic use of the adjective 烂 *lan4* 'tender' for visual dimension suggests a biological association basis for linguistic synaesthesia, as suggested by the biological association account.

(12) Tactile adjectives of hardness used for dimension (vision)

屁股 *pi4-gu3*[VISION/TARGET]	烫 *tang4*
flatus-thigh	burn
烂 *lan4*[TOUCH/SOURCE]	了 *le*
tender	ASP

'The ass was burned broken.'

There are 12 Mandarin adjectives for tactile hardness that occur with synaesthetic uses for visual situation. Some of the interpretations of synaesthetic expressions of these adjectives support the perceived similarity basis for synaesthetic transfers. As illustrated in (13a) for 僵硬 *jiang1-ying4* 'stiff', there is a correspondence concerning a negative evaluation of perceptions between the tactile sensation of strong hardness (Winter 2016a) and the visual sensation of unpleasant facial expressions. However, other synaesthetic transfers of Mandarin tactile hardness adjectives suggest a sensory integration basis for linguistic synaesthesia when used for visual situation. Example (13b) demonstrates that the visual usage of 硬 *ying4* 'hard' for hair is more likely to be grounded in the perceptual experience that thick hair generally exhibits an associating property of strong tactile hardness, which thus motivates the conceptualization of the visual situation of hair in terms of tactile concepts.

(13) Tactile adjectives of hardness used for visual situation (vision)

a.	脸部 *lian3-bu4*	**表情 *biao3-qing2***[VISION/TARGET]
	face-part	surface-emotion
	僵硬 *jiang1-ying4*[TOUCH/SOURCE]	
	stiff-hard	

'The facial expression is stiff.'

b. 一头 *yi1-tou2* **显得 *xian3-de***[VISION/TARGET]

one-CL display-ASP

粗 *cu1* **硬 *ying4***[TOUCH/SOURCE] 的 *de*

rough hard NOM

灰白 *hui1-bai2* **头发 *tou2-fa4***[VISION/TARGET]

grey-white head-hair

'the greyish white hair which seems to be thick and hard'

The ten Mandarin adjectives of tactile hardness with synaesthetic distributions in hearing all support the perceived similarity basis for linguistic synaesthesia, with respect to interpretations. As shown in (14), concepts for pleasant tactile perceptions, such as 脆 *cui4* 'crisp', were generally employed to characterize positive auditory perceptions, while concepts for unpleasant tactile perceptions, such as 僵硬 *jiang1-ying4* 'stiff', were utilized to conceptualize negative properties of auditory sensations.

(14) Tactile adjectives of hardness used for hearing

a. 一声 *yi1-sheng1* **脆 *cui4***[TOUCH/SOURCE]

one-CL crisp

响 *xiang3*[HEARING/TARGET]

sound

'a crisp sound'

b. **音色 *yin1-se4***[HEARING/TARGET] 较 *jiao4* 为 *wei2*

sound-color relatively be

僵硬 *jiang1-ying4*[TOUCH/SOURCE]

stiff-hard

'The sound is relatively stiff.'

Three adjectives of tactile hardness describe olfactory perceptions. They are 软 *ruan3* 'soft', 柔软 *rou2-ruan3* 'soft', and 轻柔 *qing1-rou2* 'soft'. In terms of the interpretation, all the olfactory usages of these three adjectives were found to characterize a pleasant odor, such as the adjective 软 *ruan3* 'soft' utilized for 香气 *xiang1-qi4* 'fragrance' in (15). Therefore, the interpretation pattern supports the perceived similarity basis for synaesthetic transfers between senses as suggested by the embodiment account. That is, tactile sensations of softness that the three adjectives originally represent are also perceptually pleasant for humans (Popova 2005; Winter 2016a).

(15) Tactile adjectives of hardness used for smell

散发 *san4-fa1*	出 *chu1*	甜 *tian2*	**软 *ruan3***[TOUCH/SOURCE]、
emit-emit	out	sweet	soft
甘 *gan1*	滑 *hua2*	与 *yu3*	果熟 *guo3-shu2*
sweet	smooth	and	fruit-mature
的 *de*	**香气 *xiang1-qi4***[SMELL/TARGET]		
NOM	fragrant-air		

'emitting sweet, soft, smooth, and ripe fragrance'

3.3.3 Sharpness

There are nine Mandarin adjectives of tactile sharpness with synaesthetic distributions. These occur only with the senses of vision and hearing, but not taste or smell.

Two Mandarin adjectives for tactile sharpness were attested with synaesthetic usages for color, of which 钝 *dun4* 'blunt' was employed for a weak light quality, and 犀利 *xi1-li4* 'sharp' describes a strong light quality, as shown in (16). The interpretations of these synaesthetic expressions support the perceived similarity basis for synaesthetic transfers from touch to vision, of which the correspondence between tactile sharpness and visual perception of light lies in perceptual intensity. It is noteworthy that the concepts 钝 *dun4* 'blunt' and 犀利 *xi1-li4* 'sharp' describe intensity rather than quality as they did in their synaesthetic uses for light. This is similar to the temperature adjective 烈 *lie4* 'scorching' used for taste (see Sect. 3.3.1).

(16) Tactile adjectives of sharpness used for color (vision)

a. 那层 *na4-ceng2* 红润 *hong2-run4*

that-CL red-moist

光泽 *guang1-ze3*[VISION/TARGET] 在 *zai4*

light-lustre ASP

钝 *dun4*[TOUCH/SOURCE] 下去 *xia4-qu4*

blunt down-go

'The red moist lustre is becoming weak.'

b. **犀利 *xi1-li4***[TOUCH/SOURCE] 而 *er2* 冰冷 *bing1-leng3*

sharp-sharp and ice-cold

曦光 *xi1-guang1*[VISION/TARGET] 中 *zhong1* 的 *de*

morning sunlight-light center NOM

背脊 *bei4-ji3*

back-backbone

'the back in the sharp and ice-cold morning sunlight'

Four Mandarin adjectives of tactile sharpness have synaesthetic uses for visual dimension. They are 尖 *jian1* 'sharp', 尖锐 *jian1-rui4* 'sharp', and 锐利 *rui4-li4* 'sharp' for high sharpness, and 钝 *dun4* 'blunt' for low sharpness. Analogous to the tactile hardness adjective 烂 *lan4* 'tender' used for visual dimension, the synaesthetic distributions of these tactile sharpness adjectives in visual dimension could also be explained by a neural association, as sharpness is also one kind of tactile perception that can be experienced by grasping. Example (17) shows that 尖 *jian1* 'sharp' was utilized to describe the shape of physical objects in the Sinica corpus.

(17) Tactile adjectives of sharpness used for dimension (vision)

尖 *jian1*[TOUCH/SOURCE] **塔 *ta3***[VISION/TARGET]

sharp tower

'the acuminate tower'

The contrast concerning affective evaluation emerge among the six adjectives of tactile sharpness in synaesthetic uses for visual situation. That is, concepts for positive high sharpness (Winter 2016a) were used to describe pleasant visual perceptions, such as 锐利 *rui4-li4* 'sharp' describing eye expressions in (18a). Concepts for unpleasant low sharpness (Winter 2016a), however, were employed for unpleasant visual sensations, such as 钝钝 *dun4-dun4* 'blunt' characterizing the numb and foolish smiles in (18b). Such a contrast is thus consistent with the perceived similarity basis for linguistic synaesthesia proposed by the embodiment account.

This contrast, however, does not appear in the synaesthetic expressions of sharpness adjectives for hearing. As demonstrated in (19), both 尖锐 *jian1-rui4* 'sharp' for positive high sharpness and 钝 *dun4* 'blunt' for negative low sharpness were used to conceptualize the unpleasant properties of auditory perceptions. In addition, there is little evidence (to my knowledge) to suggest that these synaesthetic transfers are grounded in sensory integration or neural association, which have to be left for future studies. Nevertheless, the omission of explanations for the underlying mechanism of these synaesthetic expressions would not affect the general tendency of Mandarin synaesthesia investigated by this study, since the synaesthetic examples were attested to be infrequent in the Sinica corpus (i.e., six adjectives with 145 token examples).

(18) Tactile adjectives of sharpness used for visual situation (vision)

a. **锐利 *rui4-li4***[TOUCH/SOURCE] 的 *de*

sharp-sharp NOM

目光 *mu4-guang1*[VISION/TARGET]

eye-light

'the sharp eye expression'

b. 木 *mu4* **钝钝 *dun4-dun4***[TOUCH/SOURCE] 的 *de*

numb blunt-blunt NOM

傻 *sha3* 笑 *xiao4*[VISION/TARGET]

foolish smile

'the numb, blunt, and foolish smile'

(19) Tactile adjectives of sharpness used for hearing

a. **尖锐 *jian1-rui4***[TOUCH/SOURCE] 的 *de*

sharp-sharp NOM

笛音 *di2-yin1*[HEARING/TARGET]

flute-sound

'the sharp sound of the flute'

b. **钝 *dun4***[TOUCH/SOURCE] 重 *zhong4* 沉闷 *chen2-men4*

blunt heavy deep-bored

的 *de* **碰撞声 *peng4-zhuang4-sheng1***[HEARING/TARGET]

NOM crash-crash-sound

'the blunt, heavy, and depressing sound of crashing'

3.3.4 Dampness

Mandarin adjectives of tactile dampness were found to be employed for vision, hearing, and smell, but not for taste.

There are six tactile dampness adjectives with synaesthetic uses for vision, three of them being used for color and six for visual situation, while none appearing in visual dimension. With respect to the interpretation, tactile dampness adjectives used for both color and visual situation suggest a sensory integration basis for linguistic synaesthesia. For instance, the synaesthetic use of 温润 *wen1-run4* 'moist' for color, exemplified in (20), could be grounded in the recurrent sensory association between the tactile moist texture and the gentle color of chinaware. Similarly, the adjective 湿润 *shi1-run4* 'moist' used for visual situation of the lip (21), would also be motivated by the visual perception of an amount of water on the surface of specific physical objects, which are generally associated with high tactile dampness. By contrast, the correspondences on perceived similarity between tactile dampness and color, and between tactile dampness and visual situation, are more difficult to determine in the synaesthetic examples of Mandarin tactile dampness adjectives.

(20) Tactile adjectives of dampness used for color (vision)

温润 *wen1-run4*[TOUCH/SOURCE]	的 *de*	**色泽 *se4-ze2***[VISION/TARGET]
warm-moist	NOM	color-lustre

'the gentle color'

(in the chinaware context)

(21) Tactile adjectives of dampness used for visual situation (vision)

眼看 *yan3-kan4*[VISION/TARGET]	她 *ta*	微张 *wei1-zhang1*
eye-look	she	slight-open
而 *er2*	**湿润 *shi1-run4***[TOUCH/SOURCE]	的 *de*
and	damp-moist	NOM
红唇 *hong2-chun2*[VISION/TARGET]		
red-lip		

'looking at her slightly-open and moist lip'

Synaesthetic expressions of tactile dampness adjectives for hearing are, nevertheless, consistent with the perceived similarity basis for linguistic synaesthesia. As shown in (22), the adjective for pleasant high tactile dampness (i.e., 柔润 *rou2-run4* 'soft-moist') was used for a positive auditory perception, while the adjective for unpleasant low tactile dampness (i.e., 干干 *gan1-gan1* 'dry') was employed for a negative auditory perception.

(22) Tactile adjectives of dampness used for hearing

a. 温和 *wen1-he2* ***<u>柔润 rou2-run4</u>***[TOUCH/SOURCE]

warm-harmonious soft-moist

的 *de* ***<u>声音 sheng1-yin1</u>***[HEARING/TARGET]

NOM sound-voice

'the warm, soft, and moist voice'

b. ***<u>声音 sheng1-yin1</u>***[HEARING/TARGET]

sound-voice

<u>干干 gan1-gan1</u>[TOUCH/SOURCE] 的 *de*

dry-dry PAR

'The voice is dry.'

Three tactile dampness adjectives were used for smell. One of the most interesting patterns is that dampness adjectives show the same tendency as temperature adjectives with olfactory usages (see Sect. 3.3.1). Specifically, adjectives of tactile dampness used for smell were also attested to co-occur with lexical items encoding congruent perceptions of dampness in context, such as 湿 *shi1* 'damp' co-occurring with 雨后 *yu3-hou4* 'after raining' in (23a) and 干燥 *gan1-zao4* 'dry' with 秋 *qiu1* 'autumn' in (23b). Thus, these co-occurrences would also suggest a sensory integration basis for synaesthetic transfers from tactile dampness to olfactory perceptions.

(23) Tactile adjectives of dampness used for smell

a. 雨后 *yu3-hou4* 的 *de* 天气 *tian1-qi4*

rain-after NOM sky-air

特别 *te4-bie2* 凉爽 *liang2-shuang3*， 室内 *shi4-nei4*

particularly-especially cool-bright room-in

到处 *dao4-chu4* 泛 *fan4* 着 *zhe1*

arrive-place float ASP

浓 *nong2* **<u>湿 *shi1*</u>** [TOUCH/SOURCE] 的 *de*

of intense taste damp NOM

<u>霉味 *mei2-wei4*</u> [SMELL/TARGET]

mildew-flavor

'The weather after raining is fairly cool, and there is an intense and damp smell of mildew floating in the room.'

(the co-occurring dampness-related item is: 雨后 *yu3-hou4* 'after raining')

b. 秋收 *qiu1-shou1* 结束 *jie2-shu4* 的 *de*

autumn-harvest tie-bind NOM

稻田 *dao4-tian2* 弥漫 *mi2-man4* 着 *zhe1*

rice-field pervade-pervade ASP

<u>干燥 *gan1-zao4*</u> [TOUCH/SOURCE] 的 *de*

dry-dry NOM

<u>香味 *xiang1-wei4*</u> [SMELL/TARGET]

fragrant-flavor

'The dry fragrance pervades the rice field after the autumn harvest finished.'

(the co-occurring dampness-related item is: 秋 *qiu1* 'autumn')

3.3.5 Smoothness

There are seven Mandarin adjectives for tactile smoothness with synaesthetic usages based on the Sinica corpus. Among the adjectives, one was attested with the synaesthetic distribution in taste, five in vision and hearing, and two in smell.

The only Mandarin tactile smoothness adjective used for the gustatory perception is 澀 *se4* 'rough' describing an unpleasant taste, as shown in (24). The interpretation here is consistent with the perceived similarity basis, as low tactile smoothness conceptualized by the adjective is also generally perceptually unpleasant (see Winter 2016a).

(24) Tactile adjectives of smoothness used for taste

煮 *zhu3*	去 *qu4*	**澀 *se4***[TOUCH/SOURCE]
boil	remove	rough

味 *wei4*[TASTE/TARGET]

flavor

'removing the astringent taste by boiling'

The visual usages of tactile smoothness adjectives were found for both dimension and visual situation, but not for color. As illustrated in (25), the adjective 粗 *cu1* 'rough' conceptualizes visual dimension. It should be noted here that smoothness is also one of tactile perceptions that can be experienced typically through grasping. Thus, the synaesthetic usages of Mandarin tactile smoothness adjectives for visual dimension would also be grounded in the neural association between touch and vision for shape perceptions. Therefore, it is analogous to the associations of tactile hardness and tactile sharpness with visual dimension discussed in prior sub-sections (see Sects. 3.3.2 and 3.3.3).

(25) Tactile adjectives of smoothness used for dimension (vision)

粗 *cu1*[TOUCH/SOURCE]	细 *xi4*	**线条 *xian4-tiao2***[VISION/TARGET]
rough	thin	line-line

'the thick and thin lines'

Mandarin tactile smoothness adjectives used for visual situation are grounded in two different mechanisms: Some demonstrate the sensory integration basis, while others show the perceived similarity basis for synaesthetic transfers. As illustrated in (26a), the synaesthetic use of the adjective 粗糙 *cu1-cao1* 'rough' for the visual situation of 水泥 *shui3-ni2* 'cement' is likely to be grounded in the sensory association between vision and touch, since the cement mixed with sands and stones is generally rough when touched. Nevertheless, (26b) shows that the synaesthetic use of the adjective 粗糙 *cu1-cao1* 'rough' for visual situation can only be related to a negative evaluation, as unpleasant low tactile smoothness corresponding to the crude visual situation for the adjective in touch and vision.

(26) Tactile adjectives of smoothness used for visual situation (vision)

a. **<u>眼中 *yan3-zhong1*</u>**[VISION/TARGET] 的 *de* 风景 *feng1-jing3*
eye-center NOM wind-scenery
是 *shi4* 混着 *hun4-zhe1* 沙石 *sha1-shi2* 的 *de*
be mix-ASP sand-stone NOM
<u>粗糙 *cu1-cao1*</u>[TOUCH/SOURCE] **<u>水泥 *shui3-ni2*</u>**[VISION/TARGET]
rough water-mud
'The scenery exposed to eyes is the rough cement mixed with sands and stones.'

b. 不是 *bu4-shi4* 建筑师 *jian4-zhu4-shi1* 的 *de*
NEG-be build-build-expert NOM
人们 *ren2-men1* 设计 *she4-ji4* 的 *de*
people-PL design-design NOM
<u>建筑 *jian4-zhu4*</u>[VISION/TARGET]， 它们 *ta2-men2* 的 *de*
build-build it-PL
<u>形式 *xing2-shi4*</u>[VISION/TARGET] **<u>粗糙 *cu1-cao1*</u>**[TOUCH/SOURCE]
shape-mode rough
'The appearance of the buildings which were not designed by architects is rough.'

The five Mandarin tactile smoothness adjectives with synaesthetic distributions in hearing all conceptualize low smoothness. All of their auditory uses were concerned with a negative evaluation, such as 干涩 *gan1-se4* 'dry-rough' characterizing the sad sound of howling in (27). It can thus be concluded that the synaesthetic transfers from tactile smoothness to hearing support the perceived similarity basis for linguistic synaesthesia.

(27) Tactile adjectives of smoothness used for hearing

<u>干涩 gan1-se4</u>[TOUCH/SOURCE]、	压抑 *ya1-yi4*
dry-rough	press-press
的 *de*	**<u>哀嚎 ai1-hao2</u>**[HEARING/TARGET]
NOM	sorrow-howl

'the dry-rough, depressing, and sorrow sound of howling'

Two tactile smoothness adjectives have synaesthetic distributions in smell, namely 涩 *se4* 'rough' and 滑 *hua2* 'smooth'. Based on the Sinica corpus, 涩 *se4* 'rough' was used to describe an unpleasant odor, and 滑 *hua2* 'smooth' for a pleasant odor, as shown in (28). Thus, the interpretations of the synaesthetic expressions of the two adjectives also suggest the perceived similarity basis for linguistic synaesthesia, as tactile roughness has been established to be perceptually negative for humans, while tactile smoothness is generally considered pleasant (see Winter 2016a).

(28) Tactile adjectives of smoothness used for smell

a.	霉 *mei2*	**<u>涩 se4</u>**[TOUCH/SOURCE]	**<u>气息 qi4-xi1</u>**
	mildew	rough	air-breath

'the mildewed and rough smell'

b.	散发 *san4-fa1*	出 *chu1*	甜 *tian2*	软 *ruan3*、
	emit-emit	out	sweet	soft
	甘 *gan1*	**<u>滑 hua2</u>**[TOUCH/SOURCE]	与 *yu3*	果熟 *guo3-shu2*
	sweet	smooth	and	fruit-mature
	的 *de*	**<u>香气 xiang1-qi4</u>**[SMELL/TARGET]		
	NOM	fragrant-air		

'the emitting sweet, soft, smooth, and ripe fragrance'

3.3.6 *Physical Force*

There are six Mandarin adjectives conceptualizing physical force with synaesthetic uses in the Sinica corpus. Three of them were found to have distributions in taste, six in vision, four in hearing, and two in smell.

It is interesting that all of the Mandarin adjectives of physical force conceptualize perceptual intensity when used for the gustatory perception, for color in the visual domain, and for auditory and olfactory perception. As shown in (29), 强劲 *qiang2-jing4* 'of strong force' was employed to denote the strong taste of tea, while 轻 *qing1* 'light (in weight)' describes the weakness of the spicy taste. Similarly, 重 *zhong4* 'heavy' for high physical force was used for the high perceptual intensity experienced by the visual sense for color as in (30a), by the auditory sense as in (31a), and by the olfactory sense as in (32a). Concepts for low physical force, such as 轻 *qing1* 'light (in weight)', were utilized for low perceptual intensity, as illustrated in (30b), (31b), and (32b). The interpretation patterns of physical force adjectives in synaesthetic uses thus support the perceived similarity basis for linguistic synaesthesia, as suggested by the embodiment account.

(29) Tactile adjectives of physical force used for taste

a. **茶汤 *cha2-tang1***$_{\text{[TASTE/TARGET]}}$ **强劲 *qiang2-jing4***$_{\text{[TOUCH/SOURCE]}}$

tea-soup strong-strength

'The taste of tea is strong.'

b. **轻 *qing1***$_{\text{[TOUCH/SOURCE]}}$ **辣 *la4***$_{\text{[TASTE/TARGET]}}$

light (in weight) hot (in taste)

'the light spicy'

(30) Tactile adjectives of physical force used for color (vision)

a. **<u>发色 *fa4-se4*</u>**[VISION/TARGET] 也 ye3 不能 *bu4-neng3*

hair-color too NEG-AUX

太 *tai4* **<u>重 *zhong4*</u>**[TOUCH/SOURCE]

too heavy

'The color of hair cannot be too heavy.'

b. 灌木 *guan4-mu4* 丛 *cong2* 的 *de*

bush-wood bosk NOM

<u>轻 *qing1*</u>[TOUCH/SOURCE] **<u>绿 *lv4*</u>**[VISION/TARGET]

light (in weight) green

'the light green of the bosk'

(31) Tactile adjectives of physical force used for hearing

a. **<u>重重 *zhong4-zhong4*</u>**[TOUCH/SOURCE] 的 *de*

heavy-heavy NOM

<u>琴音 *qin2-yin1*</u>[HEARING/TARGET]

lyre-sound

'the heavy sound of the lyre'

b. **轻 *qing1***[TOUCH/SOURCE] **声 *sheng1***[HEARING/TARGET] 喊 *han3*

light (in weight) sound shout

起來 *qi3-lai2*

up-come

'to shout using a light voice'

(32) Tactile adjectives of physical force used for smell

a. **煤味 *mei2-wei4***[SMELL/TARGET] 太 *tai4* **重 *zhong4***[TOUCH/SOURCE]

coal-flavor too heavy

'The smell of coal is too heavy.'

b. **轻 *qing1***[TOUCH/SOURCE] 淡 *dan4*

light (in weight) of mild taste

香气 *xiang1-qi4*[SMELL/TARGET]

fragrant-air

'the light and mild fragrance'

Synaesthetic uses of physical force adjectives for visual situation, however, cannot be explained exclusively by the perceived similarity basis. As demonstrated in (33a), some synaesthetic uses of the adjective 轻 *qing1* 'light (in weight)' can be motivated by the correspondence in low perceptual intensity between the physical force and the visual perception of a geometric line. Example (33b), however, illustrates that other synaesthetic usages of the adjective 轻 *qing1* 'light (in weight)' for visual situation would be grounded in sensory integration, as the buoyant visual situation of gauze is generally associated with a light weight.

(33) Tactile adjectives of physical force used for visual situation (vision)

a. 在 *zai4* 几何学 *ji3-he2-xue2* 上 *shang4* […]

in geometry up […]

轻 *qing1*[TOUCH/SOURCE] 细 *xi4* 之 *zhi1*

light (in weight) thin NOM

线 *xian4*[VISION/TARGET] 具有 *ju4-you3* 纤细 *xian1-xi4*、

line possess-have thin-thin

柔弱 *rou2-ruo4*、 轻巧 *qing1-qiao3*、

soft-weak light (in weight)-delicate

潇洒 *xiao1-sa3* 的 *de*

(of water) deep and clear-spill NOM

感觉 *gan3-jue3*

feel-feel

'In geometry (…), the light and thin line gives the thin, weak, delicate, and natural feeling.'

b. 校园 *xiao4-yuan2* 中 *zhong1* 不时 *bu4-shi2*

school-campus center NEG-time

可 *ke3* **见 *jian4***[VISION/TARGET] 一袭 *yi1-xi2*

AUX see one-CL

轻 *qing1*[TOUCH/SOURCE] **纱 *sha1***[VISION/TARGET]

light (in weight) gauze

'The light gauze can often be seen in the campus.'

3.3.7 Pain

There are four Mandarin adjectives for pain attested with synaesthetic uses in the Sinica corpus. One of the adjectives exhibits distributions in taste, three in vision, one in hearing, and none in smell.

The gustatory usage of the adjective 麻 *ma2* 'trembling', as shown in (34), is consistent with the physiological finding that the sensation induced on the tongue and lips by Szechuan pepper shares the same RA1 channel with mechanical vibration (Hagura et al. 2013). Therefore, the adjective 麻 *ma2* 'trembling' used for taste suggests the neural association basis for linguistic synaesthesia, as assumed by the biological association account.

(34) Tactile adjectives of pain used for taste

干煸 *gan1-bian3*		**牛肉丝 *niu2-rou4-si1***[TASTE/TARGET],	
dry-fry		cow-meet-slice	
麻 *ma2*[TOUCH/SOURCE]	而 *er2*	不 *bu4*	辣 *la4*
trembling	but	NEG	hot (in taste)

'The dry-fried slice of beef is pungent, but not hot.'

There is only one Mandarin pain adjective with synaesthetic usages for visual dimension (i.e., 胀 *zhang4* 'swelling [in pain]'), and two for visual situation, while none appearing for color. As shown in (35), the adjective 胀 *zhang4* 'swelling (in pain)' used for visual dimension denotes the enlargement of shapes, as swelling is generally associated with pain. Thus, the synaesthetic use of the adjective 胀 *zhang4* 'swelling (in pain)' for visual dimension suggests a sensory integration basis for synaesthetic transfers. Example (36), however, shows that the synaesthetic uses of Mandarin pain adjectives for visual situation are in line with the perceived similarity basis for linguistic synaesthesia, as the tactile stabbing sensation and the visual glaring sensation conceptualized by 刺刺*ci4-ci4* 'stabbing' are both unpleasant.

(35) Tactile adjectives of pain used for dimension (vision)

发 *fa1*	**胀 *zhang4***[TOUCH/SOURCE]	的 *de*
produce	swelling (in pain)	NOM
罐头 *guan4-tou2*[VISION/TARGET]		
tin-head		

'the swelling tin'

(36) Tactile adjectives of pain used for visual situation (vision)

刺刺 *ci4-ci4*[TOUCH/SOURCE]	的 *de*、	不 *bu4*
stabbing- stabbing	NOM	NEG
太 *tai4*	舒服 *shu1-fu1*	的 *de*
too	stretch-dress	NOM
视觉 *shi4-jue2*	**效果 *xiao4-guo3***[VISION/TARGET]	
vision-sense	effect-result	

'the stabbing and uncomfortable visual effect'

The only Mandarin pain adjective with auditory uses is 软弱 *ruan3-ruo4* 'feeble', conceptualizing a low intensity of hearing, as shown in (37). This interpretation would support the sensory integration basis for linguistic synaesthesia, as humans experiencing feeble sensations generally produce weak voices.

(37) Tactile adjectives of pain used for hearing

以 *yi3*	**软弱 *ruan3-ruo4***[TOUCH/SOURCE]	的 *de*
use	soft-weak	NOM
声音 *sheng1-yin1*[HEARING/TARGET]		道 *dao4*
sound-voice		say

'saying in a weak voice'

3.3.8 Summary

It has been demonstrated that Mandarin adjectives for specific tactile perceptions exhibit more complex patterns in linguistic synaesthesia than the adjectives for tactile intensities do. Specifically, Mandarin adjectives for tactile hardness, sharpness, smoothness, and pain were identified with synaesthetic uses for visual dimension, while adjectives for tactile intensity were not found to show the same distribution. In addition, Mandarin tactile quality adjectives exhibit different tendencies from tactile intensity adjectives, as there are tactile quality adjectives that conceptualize perceptual intensity rather than a specific perceptual property in their synaesthetic expressions, such as the Mandarin temperature adjective 烈 *lie4* 'scorching' used for taste. However, there is no tactile intensity adjective found to denote perceptual properties in linguistic synaesthesia; instead, all preserve their intensity concepts.

It should also be noted that the general synaesthetic distributions of Mandarin tactile quality adjectives are consistent with the prediction of the embodiment account, analogous to those of Mandarin tactile intensity adjectives. Nevertheless, Mandarin adjectives for specific tactile perceptions do show differences in their synaesthetic transfers. One intriguing pattern is that adjectives representing tactile perceptions that are typically experienced by grasping, such as hardness and smoothness, demonstrate synaesthetic transfers to visual dimension, whereas adjectives of other tactile perceptions (e.g., temperature and dampness adjectives) do not show this tendency. Furthermore, in terms of the underlying mechanisms of linguistic synaesthesia, the perceived similarity of intensity and affective evaluation proposed in the embodiment account of linguistic synaesthesia has been found to be insufficient to explain the synaesthetic usages of tactile quality adjectives. Rather, sensory integration and neural association have also been found in instances of linguistic synaesthesia in Mandarin tactile quality adjectives.

3.4 Synaesthetic Tendencies of Mandarin Tactile Adjectives

This chapter has explored the synaesthetic tendencies of Mandarin tactile adjectives based on their distributions in the Sinica corpus. As predicted by the embodiment account of linguistic synaesthesia, Mandarin tactile adjectives were used for four senses (i.e., taste, vision, hearing, and smell). However, Mandarin adjectives for different tactile perceptions show different patterns in linguistic synaesthesia. This difference in patterns was not predicted by the embodiment account, as the theory only focuses on five sensory modalities, but not on sub-domains of senses.

Synaesthetic transfers of Mandarin tactile adjectives could be motivated not only by perceived similarity, but also by sensory integration and neural association. The patterns are thus consistent with the assumption of Zhao et al. (2018b) that linguistic synaesthesia would most likely be grounded in multiple mechanisms.

The tendencies of linguistic synaesthesia of tactile adjectives will be compared with those of gustatory, visual, auditory, and olfactory adjectives in the following two chapters, to examine the general directional tendencies of Mandarin synaesthesia. The next chapter will focus on the synaesthetic patterns of gustatory adjectives, based on which the directionality pattern between touch and taste for linguistic synaesthesia in Mandarin will be determined.

References

Amedi, Amir, Gilad Jacobson, Talma Hendler, Rafael Malach, and Ehud Zohary. 2002. Convergence of visual and tactile shape processing in the human lateral occipital complex. *Cerebral Cortex* 12 (11): 1202–1212.

Caterina, Michael, Mark Schumacher, Makoto Tominaga, Tobias Rosen, Jon Levine, and David Julius. 1997. The capsaicin receptor: A heat-activated ion channel in the pain pathway. *Nature* 389 (6653): 816–824.

Chen, Keh-Jiann, Chu-Ren Huang, Li-Ping Chang and Hui-Li Hsu. 1996. Sinica corpus: Design methodology for balanced corpora. *Proceedings of the 11th Pacific Asia conference on language, information and computation (PACLIC 11)*, 167–176.

Hagura, Nobuhiro, Harry Barber, and Patrick Haggard. 2013. Food vibrations: Asian spice sets lips trembling. *Proceedings of the Royal Society of London B: Biological Sciences* 280: 1–6.

Hirasa, Kenji, and Mitsuo Takemasa. 1998. *Spice science and technology*. New York: Marcel Dekker Inc.

Kennedy, Christopher. 1999. Gradable adjectives denote measure functions, not partial functions. *Studies in the Linguistic Sciences* 29 (1): 65–80.

Kennedy, Christopher, and Louise McNally. 2005. Scale structure, degree modification, and the semantics of gradable predicates. *Language* 81 (2): 345–381.

Kennedy, Christopher, and Louise McNally. 2009. Color, context, and compositionality. *Synthese* 174 (1): 79–98.

Lehrer, Adrienne. 1985. Markedness and antonymy. *Journal of Linguistics* 21 (2): 397–429.

Lehrer, Adrienne, and Keith Lehrer. 1982. Antonymy. *Linguistics and Philosophy* 5 (4): 483–501.

Marks, Lawrence E. 1978. *The unity of the senses: Interrelations among the modalities*. New York: Academic Press.

Paradis, Carita, and Mats Eeg-Olofsson. 2013. Describing sensory experience: The genre of wine reviews. *Metaphor and Symbol* 28 (1): 22–40.

Popova, Y. 2005. Image schemas and verbal synaesthesia. In *From perception to meaning: Image schema in cognitive linguistics*, ed. B. Hampe and J.E. Grady, 395–420., (Cognitive Linguistics Research 29) Berlin and New York: Mouton de Gruyter.

Rakova, Marina. 2003. *The extent of the literal: Metaphor, polysemy and the theories of concepts*. Hampshire: Palgrave Macmillan.

Shen, Yeshayahu. 1997. Cognitive constraints on poetic figures. *Cognitive Linguistics* 8 (1): 33–71.

Spence, Charles. 2011. Crossmodal correspondences: A tutorial review. *Attention, Perception, & Psychophysics* 73 (4): 971–995.

Williams, Joseph. 1976. Synaesthetic adjectives: A possible law of sematic change. *Language* 52 (2): 461–478.

Winter, Bodo. 2016a. *The sensory structure of the English lexicon*. Merced dissertation, Merced, CA: University of California.

Wyszecki, Günter, and W.S. Stiles. 1967. *Color Science: Concepts and methods, quantitative data and formulae*. New York: Wiley.

Zhao, Qingqing, Chu-Ren Huang, and Yunfei Long. 2018b. Synaesthesia in Chinese: A corpus-based study on gustatory adjectives in Mandarin. *Linguistics* 56 (5): 1167–1194.

Chapter 4
Mandarin Gustatory Adjectives

This chapter is extension of Zhao et al. (2018b) to explore the finer-grained tendencies and mechanisms of synaesthetic usages of Mandarin gustatory adjectives. In addition, it differs from Zhao et al.'s (2018b) contrastive study focusing on the variations of synaesthetic patterns between Mandarin and English concerning gustatory adjectives. In addition, more synaesthetic data has been collected in this study, by adopting a looser criterion for identifying Mandarin adjectives originally used for taste. For instance, the Mandarin adjective 腻 *ni4* 'greasy' has the etymological meaning of 'much fat' in 说文解字 *Shuo1-wen2 jie3-zi4*. It is analogous to the Mandarin adjective 浓 *nong2* 'dense dew' (see Sect. 2.1.1 in Chap. 2), with respect to both taste and vision being possible original source domains. 浓 *nong2* 'dense dew' could be assigned to taste, based on its close relation with the attested gustatory adjective 淡 *dan4* 'not salty/of mild taste'. However, there is no attested gustatory item related to 腻 *ni4* 'greasy'. This study, nevertheless, includes 腻 *ni4* 'greasy' as an original gustatory item, on the basis of its more frequent use for taste (i.e., 18 counts) than for vision (i.e., three counts) in Mandarin based on the Sinica corpus.

Sections 4.1 and 4.2 of this chapter will explore the synaesthetic tendencies for Mandarin gustatory intensity adjectives and Mandarin gustatory quality adjectives respectively. The general transfer patterns and underlying mechanisms of linguistic synaesthesia in Mandarin gustatory adjectives will be discussed in Sect. 4.3. The last section will examine the directionality between touch and taste in Mandarin synaesthesia.

Q. Zhao, *Embodied Conceptualization or Neural Realization*,
Frontiers in Chinese Linguistics 10, https://doi.org/10.1007/978-981-32-9315-1_4

4.1 Gustatory Adjectives of Intensity

There are 21 Mandarin gustatory adjectives identified with synaesthetic usages in the Sinica corpus, with 2291 token examples (see Appendix B). Among these adjectives, two adjectives conceptualize gustatory intensity: 淡 *dan4* 'not salty/of mild taste' and 浓 *nong2* 'of intense taste'.[1]

Gustatory intensity adjectives were used for vision, hearing, and smell, but not for touch in the Sinica corpus, as shown in examples (1) through (4).

(1) Gustatory adjectives of intensity used for color (vision)

a. **淡 *dan4***[TASTE/SOURCE] **蓝色 *lan2-se4***[VISION/TARGET]

of mild taste blue-color

'light blue'

b. **叶色 *ye4-se4***[VISION/TARGET] **浓 *nong2***[TASTE/SOURCE]

leave-color of intense taste

绿 *lv4*[VISION/TARGET]

green

'The color of leaves is deep-green.'

[1]The adjective 淡 *dan4* 'not salty/of mild taste' can be used both for gustatory quality, such as 菜不咸不淡 *cai4 bu4 xian2 bu4 dan4* 'the dish is not salty or tasteless (just right)', and gustatory intensity, such as 淡淡的甜味 *dan4-dan4 de tian2 wei4* 'the slight sweetness' in Mandarin. Moreover, the gustatory quality use is predominant for the adjective 淡 *dan4* in Mandarin, with about 85.6% (161/188) of its gustatory usages being for quality in the Sinica corpus. However, the adjective used in synaesthetic expressions was attested to always denote the perceptual intensity for other sensory modalities. Thus, the adjective is assigned to the category of gustatory intensity adjectives in this discussion.

(2) Gustatory adjectives of intensity used for visual situation (vision)

a. **淡淡 *dan4-dan4***[TASTE/SOURCE] **笑意 *xiao4-yi4***[VISION/TARGET]

of mild taste-of mild taste smile-meaning

'the faint smile'

b. **浓浓 *nong2-nong2***[TASTE/SOURCE] 的 *de*

of intense taste-of intense taste NOM

眉毛 *mei2-mao2*[VISION/TARGET]

eyebrow-hair

'the thick eyebrow'

(3) Gustatory adjectives of intensity used for hearing

a. **淡 *dan4***[TASTE/SOURCE] 了 *le*

of mild taste ASP

喧闹声 *xuan1-nao4-sheng1*[HEARING/TARGET]

clamor-noisy-sound

'The noise is weakened.'

b. **浓浓 *nong2-nong2***[TASTE/SOURCE]

of intense taste-of intense taste

广东腔 *guang3dong1-qiang1*[HEARING/TARGET]

Guangdong-accent

'the strong accent of Cantonese'

(4) Gustatory adjectives of intensity used for smell

a. **淡淡 *dan4-dan4***[TASTE/SOURCE] 的 *de*

of mild taste-of mild taste NOM

花香 *hua1-xiang1*[SMELL/TARGET]

flower-fragrance

'the light fragrance of flowers'

b. 女子 *nv3-zi3* 的 *de* **体味 *ti3-wei4***[SMELL/TARGET]

female-PAR GEN body-odor

真 *zhen1* **浓 *nong2***[TASTE/SOURCE]

really of intense taste

'The odor of the woman is quite strong.'

The synaesthetic distributions of Mandarin adjectives of gustatory intensity are consistent with the prediction of the embodiment account of linguistic synaesthesia. That is, all synaesthetic usages of Mandarin gustatory intensity adjectives follow the trend from more embodied to less embodied, namely, from the sense that needs physical contact with perceived objects (taste) to the senses that don't (vision, hearing, and smell). The unobserved direction from taste to touch is also predicted by the theory. According to Lehrer (1978) and Shen (1997), touch is more embodied than taste due to the number of sensory receptors (all over the body vs. only in the mouth).

The interpretations of synaesthetic expressions for these gustatory intensity adjectives also support the perceived similarity basis for linguistic synaesthesia proposed by the embodiment account. That is, the concept of intensity and the polarity of the intensity scale for the adjectives 淡 *dan4* 'of mild taste' and 浓 *nong2* 'of intense taste' are both preserved in synaesthetic transfers. Specifically speaking, 淡 *dan4* 'of mild taste', originally on the lower side of the intensity scale for gustation, was employed to characterize faintness of perceptions in vision, hearing, and smell, as illustrated in (1a), (2a), (3a), and (4a), whereas 浓 *nong2* 'of intense taste' on the higher side of the gustatory intensity scale, retained strongness in what was perceived by the eyes, ears, and the nose, such as (1b), (2b), (3b), and (4b).

It is interesting to note that Mandarin gustatory intensity adjectives were not attested to exhibit synaesthetic uses for visual dimension. I will return to the issue that synaesthetic transfers to visual dimension are restricted to tactile grasping-based sensations in Chapt. 7.

4.2 Gustatory Adjectives of Quality

Mandarin gustatory quality adjectives were found with synaesthetic uses for vision, hearing, and smell in the Sinica corpus, just as the Mandarin gustatory intensity adjectives discussed above.

There are ten Mandarin gustatory adjectives of quality that have synaesthetic distributions in vision. Among these adjectives, five were employed to characterize color, and nine to describe visual situation. None appeared with synaesthetic uses for visual dimension. Therefore, Mandarin gustatory quality adjectives, similar to Mandarin gustatory intensity adjectives, were also unattested to exhibit a synaesthetic transfer to visual dimension.

The interpretations of synaesthetic expressions for Mandarin gustatory quality adjectives used for color and visual situation both support the perceived similarity basis for linguistic synaesthesia as suggested by the embodiment account. Specifically, the adjectives with color usages all originally conceptualize positive tastes, which were still employed to describe pleasant visual sensations of specific colors, such as 鲜美 *xian1-mei3* 'tasty' in (5). With respect to Mandarin gustatory quality adjectives used for visual situation, affective evaluation is also retained. For instance, 甜 *tian2* 'sweet' always implies that the objects observed are pleasing to the eye, as in (6a), whereas 苦 *ku3* 'bitter' indicates an unpleasant visual perception, as illustrated in (6b).

(5) Gustatory adjectives of quality used for color (vision)

颜色 *yan2-se4*[VISION/TARGET]	**鲜美 *xian1-mei3***[TASTE/SOURCE]
face-color	tasty-tasty

'The color is bright and beautiful.'

(6) Gustatory adjectives of quality used for visual situation (vision)

a.	**甜美 *tian2-mei3***[TASTE/SOURCE]	的 *de*
	sweet-tasty	NOM
	笑容 *xiao4-rong2*[VISION/TARGET]	
	smile-appearance	

'the sweet smile'

b.	**苦 *ku3***[TASTE/SOURCE]	着 *zhe1*	**脸 *lian3***[VISION/TARGET]
	bitter	ASP	face

'with bitter facial expressions'

The correspondence concerning affective evaluation between taste and hearing is also attested for the nine Mandarin gustatory quality adjectives used for auditory perceptions. As illustrated in (7), 甜 *tian2* 'sweet' characterizes a positive auditory sensation, while 苦 *ku3* 'bitter' describes an unpleasant perception in hearing. Thus, the synaesthetic transfers from taste to hearing for Mandarin gustatory quality adjectives are also consistent with the perceived similarity of subjective evaluation underlying linguistic synaesthesia, as suggested by the embodiment account.

(7) Gustatory adjectives of quality used for hearing

a. <u>**甜 *tian2***</u>[TASTE/SOURCE] 而 *er2* 轻柔 *qing1-rou2*

sweet and light-soft

的 *de* <u>**声音 *sheng1-yin1***</u>[HEARING/TARGET]

NOM voice-voice

'the sweet and soft voice'

b. <u>**苦 *ku3***</u>[TASTE/SOURCE] <u>**调 *diao4***</u>[HEARING/TARGET]

bitter tune

'the bitter tune'

There are 14 Mandarin gustatory quality adjectives with synaesthetic usages for olfactory perceptions. Zhao et al. (2018b) have suggested that the olfactory usages of Mandarin gustatory quality adjectives are grounded in the perceived similarity of affective evaluation between taste and smell. For instance, the adjective 甜 *tian2* 'sweet' as a positive taste was generally used for a pleasant perception of smell in the Sinica corpus, as shown in (8a) for 香 *xiang1* 'fragrance'. In addition, the study also assumed that the collocations of the adjectives 苦 *ku3* 'bitter' and 酸 *suan1* 'sour', both of which conceptualize negative perceptions of taste, with 香 *xiang1* 'fragrance' were triggered by specific contexts, i.e., tea or coffee and vinegar respectively, as illustrated in (8b) and (8c). However, the contextually-triggered olfactory uses of Mandarin gustatory quality adjectives in fact indicate the sensory integration basis for linguistic synaesthesia. That is, the bitter taste as an intrinsic property of coffee and tea tends to be perceptually associated with the odor of these objects, as tasting and smelling are generally mutually-dependent to determine the flavor of food (Winter 2016a, b). Thus, the conceptualization of the olfactory perception of coffee and tea in terms of the concepts of the gustatory perceptions of these objects is motivated. Similarly, the recurring association between the sour taste (as an intrinsic property of vinegar) and the odor of vinegar is also likely to ground the description of olfactory properties of vinegar through its gustatory concepts.

(8) Gustatory adjectives of quality used for smell

a. **扑鼻 *pu1-bi2***[SMELL/TARGET] 的 *de*

rush.to-nose NOM

甜 *tian2*[TASTE/SOURCE] **香 *xiang1***[SMELL/TARGET]

sweet fragrant

'the tangy sweet fragrance'

b. 微 *wei1* **苦 *ku3***[TASTE/SOURCE]

slightly bitter

气香 *qi1-xiang1*[SMELL/TARGET]

air-fragrant

'the slightly bitter fragrance of air' (in the coffee context)

c. **酸 *suan1*** [TASTE/SOURCE] **香 *xiang1***[SMELL/TARGET]

sour fragrant

扑鼻 *pu1-bi2*[SMELL/TARGET]

rush.to-nose

'The pleasant sour odor is strong.' (in the vinegar context)

Mandarin gustatory quality adjectives have been found not only to exhibit transfers from taste to less embodied modalities, including vision, hearing, and smell, as predicted by the embodiment account, but also to be employed for touch, the more embodied modality.

There are five Mandarin gustatory quality adjectives identified with synaesthetic transfers to touch, involving 104 token examples, and illustrated in (9). In terms of the interpretation, the adjectives 酸 *suan1* 'sour', 腻 *ni4* 'greasy', 油腻 *you2-ni4* 'greasy', and 苦 *ku3* 'bitter', conceptualizing unpleasant gustatory perceptions originally, were still used to characterize negative sensations in touch, as in (9a–d).

These examples therefore support the perceived similarity basis for synaesthetic transfers, as suggested by the embodiment account.

The gustatory adjective 辣 *la4* 'hot (in taste)', however, shows a different pattern. The adjective conceptualizes a neutral gustatory perception, generated when the tongue is in contact with a chilli pepper in Mandarin (Zhao et al. 2018b). Studies such as Wu (1989) and Wang (1996) have demonstrated that the adjective 辣 *la4* 'hot (in taste)' is a later use of 辛 *xin1* 'hot (in taste)', originally related to taste. Thus, the adjective 辣 *la4* 'hot (in taste)' is different from English gustatory adjectives *pungent* and *hot* that describe gustation through the synaesthetic transfers from touch (Williams 1976; Rakova 2003). With respect to the tactile use of 辣 *la4* 'hot (in taste)', it conceptualizes a combinative perception of high temperature and pain, as shown in (9e). Therefore, the interpretation of 辣 *la4* 'hot (in taste)' used for touch is in line with the biological association of a spicy taste with temperature (Hirasa and Takemasa 1998) and pain (Caterina et al. 1997). Thus, the synaesthetic usage of the gustatory quality adjective 辣 *la4* 'hot (in taste)' for touch supports the biological association basis for linguistic synaesthesia, as proposed by the biological association account.

(9) Gustatory adjectives of quality used for touch

a.	觉得 *jue2-de*	**鼻子 *bi2-zi***[TOUCH/TARGET]
	feel-receive	nose-PAR
	一 *yi1*	**酸 *suan1***[TASTE/SOURCE]
	ASP	sour
	'feeling sore in the nose'	
b.	**一身 *yi1-shen1***[TOUCH/TARGET]	**腻 *ni4***[TASTE/SOURCE]
	one-body	greasy'
	汗 *han4*[TOUCH/TARGET]	
	sweat	
	'the sticky sweat all over the body'	

c.	不 *bu4*	**油腻 *you3-ni4*** [TASTE/SOURCE]	的 *de*
	NEG	oil-greasy	NOM
	珍珠 *zhen1-zhu1*	香水 *xiang1-shui3*	
	pearl-pearl	fragrant-water	
	洗面霜 *xi3-mian4-shuang1* [TOUCH/TARGET]		
	wash-face-cream		
	'the non-greasy cleansing cream with pearl essence and perfume'		
d.	**苦 *ku3*** [TASTE/SOURCE]	**寒 *han3*** [TOUCH/TARGET]	
	bitter	cold	
	'bitter cold'		
e.	感觉 *gan3-jue2*	**眼 *yan3*** [TOUCH/TARGET]	
	feel-feel	eye	
	辣 *la4* [TASTE/SOURCE]	手 *shou3*	冷 *leng3*
	hot (in taste)	hand	cold
	'feeling burning pain in eyes and cold in hands'		

4.3 Synaesthetic Tendencies of Mandarin Gustatory Adjectives

Mandarin gustatory intensity and quality adjectives were found to show subtle differences in linguistic synaesthesia. Specifically, the embodiment account predicts all synaesthetic transfers of gustatory intensity adjectives, as they follow the embodiment principle of mapping from the more embodied modality (i.e., taste) to less embodied ones (i.e., vision, hearing, and smell). In addition, the interpretations of synaesthetic expressions of these intensity adjectives are all consistent with the perceived similarity basis for linguistic synaesthesia, as suggested by the embodiment account. However, Mandarin gustatory quality adjectives exhibit more complex patterns, compared to Mandarin gustatory intensity adjectives. Though most of the synaesthetic distributions of Mandarin gustatory quality adjectives follow the embodiment tendency mapping from the more embodied to the less embodied, there are a small but important number of exceptions to the embodiment account mapping from taste to touch. The exceptions account for 26.3% (5/19) by type and 6.0% (104/1738) by token among all synaesthetic usages of Mandarin gustatory quality adjectives. With respect to the underlying mechanisms of linguistic synaesthesia, apart from the perceived similarity basis, there are synaesthetic expressions of Mandarin gustatory quality adjectives suggesting a sensory integration basis (e.g., the olfactory usages of 苦 *ku3* 'bitter' and 酸 *suan1* 'sour') and a biological association basis (e.g., the adjective 辣 *la4* 'hot [in taste]' used for touch).

It is notable, however, that Mandarin gustatory intensity adjectives also demonstrate similarities with Mandarin gustatory quality adjectives. That is, both the intensity adjectives and the quality adjectives were not used for visual dimension. It can thus be concluded that Mandarin gustatory adjectives were unattested to show the synaesthetic transfer to the visual modality dimension.

There are other general synaesthetic patterns exhibited by Mandarin gustatory adjectives when the tendencies of Mandarin gustatory intensity and quality adjectives in linguistic synaesthesia are combined. Specifically, most synaesthetic distributions of Mandarin gustatory adjectives, specifically 76.2% (16/21) for lexical types and 95.5% (2187/2291) for lexical tokens, are consistent with the embodiment account prediction of linguistic synaesthesia mapping from the more embodied to the less embodied. However, there is a significant portion of Mandarin gustatory adjectives—23.8% (5/21) by type and 4.5% (104/2291) by token—violating the embodiment principle with transfers from taste to touch. With respect to the underlying mechanism of linguistic synaesthesia, Mandarin gustatory adjectives not only show a perceived similarity basis, but also demonstrate a sensory integration basis and a biological association basis for linguistic synaesthesia. Hence, Mandarin gustatory adjectives are analogous to Mandarin tactile adjectives in terms of underlying mechanisms for linguistic synaesthesia (see Chap. 3).

4.4 Directionality Between Touch and Taste

There are basically two methods proposed to determine the synaesthetic directionality between sensory modalities in the literature. One is Strik Lievers' (2015) study utilizing the frequency of synaesthetic transfers in a specific corpus, and the other is Zhao and Huang's (2018) work focusing on the percentage of synaesthetic lexical types in one sense used for another sense. As pointed by Winter (2016a), both token and type should be considered for the synaesthetic directionality. This study takes into consideration both the frequency of synaesthetic tokens and the percentage of synaesthetic lexical types to explore the directional tendency between touch and taste for Mandarin synaesthesia.

Specifically, the synaesthetic transfers from touch to taste show a similar frequency to transfers from taste to touch in the Sinica corpus, with 125 token examples (see Appendix A) and 104 token examples (see Appendix B) respectively. In terms of the percentage of synaesthetic lexical types, 9.6% (7/73) of Mandarin tactile synaesthetic adjectives were used for taste, and 23.8% (5/21) of

TOUCH ⟷ TASTE

Fig. 4.1 Directional tendencies between touch and taste in Mandarin synaesthesia

Mandarin gustatory synaesthetic adjectives were employed for touch. Although the taste-for-touch percentage is larger than the touch-for-taste, both percentages are much smaller than 50%, which makes it difficult to determine with certainty a predominant transfer direction between touch and taste. Therefore, this study has generalized the directional tendency between touch and taste for Mandarin synaesthesia as Fig. 4.1.

In conclusion, the predominant directionality from touch to taste observed in Indo-European languages, such as English, French, and Italian (see Ullmann 1957; Williams 1976; Strik Lievers 2015), was not attested for Mandarin synaesthesia, based on both lexical tokens and lexical types. It is intriguing that Zhao and Huang (2018) also pointed out the bi-directionality between touch and taste for Mandarin synaesthesia, although the study utilized a different method (i.e., the dictionary-based approach).

One of the most important implications with respect to the different directional tendency between touch and taste for Mandarin synaesthesia from that in Indo-European languages is that Mandarin synaesthesia would not support the cross-lingual universality of synaesthetic tendencies hypothesized by the biological association account of linguistic synaesthesia (Williams 1976). I will return to this issue in more detail in Chap. 7, after determining the synaesthetic tendencies of Mandarin visual, auditory, and olfactory adjectives, as well as Mandarin compound adjectives combining different sensory modalities.

References

Caterina, Michael, Mark Schumacher, Makoto Tominaga, Tobias Rosen, Jon Levine, and David Julius. 1997. The capsaicin receptor: A heat-activated ion channel in the pain pathway. *Nature* 389(6653): 816–824.

Hirasa, Kenji, and Mitsuo Takemasa. 1998. *Spice science and technology*. New York: Marcel Dekker Inc.

Lehrer, Adrienne. 1978. Structures of the lexicon and transfer of meaning. *Lingua* 45(2): 95–123.

Rakova, Marina. 2003. *The extent of the literal: Metaphor, polysemy and the theories of concepts*. Hampshire: Palgrave Macmillan.

Shen, Yeshayahu. 1997. Cognitive constraints on poetic figures. *Cognitive Linguistics* 8(1): 33–71.

Strik Lievers, Francesca. 2015. Synaesthesia: A corpus-based study of cross-modal directionality. *Functions of Language* 22(1): 69–95.

Ullmann, Stephen. 1957. *The principles of semantics*. Oxford: Basil Blackwell.

Wang, Ning (王宁). 1996. *The principle in etymological studies on Chinese* [训诂学原理]. Beijing [北京]: China International Radio Press [中国国际广播出版社].

Williams, Joseph. 1976. Synaesthetic adjectives: A possible law of sematic change. *Language* 52 (2): 461–478.

Winter, Bodo. 2016a. *The sensory structure of the English lexicon*. Merced dissertation. Merced, CA: University of California.

Winter, Bodo. 2016b. Taste and smell words form an affectively loaded and emotionally flexible part of the English lexicon. *Language, Cognition and Neuroscience* 31(8): 975–988.

Wu, Tieping (伍铁平). 1989. Different categorizations to the world through gustatory and temperature words in different languages—A typological study [不同语言的味觉词和温度词对客观现实的不同切分——语言类型学研究]. *Language Teaching and Linguistic Studies* [语言教学与研究] 1(1): 120–137.

Zhao, Qingqing (赵青青) and Chu-Ren Huang (黄居仁). 2018. Mapping models and underlying mechanisms of synaesthetic metaphors in Mandarin [现代汉语通感隐喻的映射模型与制约机制]. *Language Teaching and Linguistic Studies* [语言教学与研究] 1: 44–55.

Zhao, Qingqing, Chu-Ren Huang, and Yunfei Long. 2018b. Synaesthesia in Chinese: A corpus-based study on gustatory adjectives in Mandarin. *Linguistics* 56(5): 1167–1194.

Chapter 5
Mandarin Visual, Auditory, and Olfactory Adjectives

The synaesthetic data from the Sinica corpus shows that vision, hearing, and smell exhibit much lower degrees of synaesthetic participation than touch and taste in Mandarin (see Chap. 2). In addition, there are only four auditory adjectives and two olfactory adjectives identified with synaesthetic uses (see Chap. 2). This chapter focuses on the synaesthetic tendencies of Mandarin adjectives from three sensory modalities (i.e., vision, hearing, and smell).

Shen (1997) has suggested that vision, hearing, and smell do not necessarily involve physical contact between sensory organs and perceived objects and therefore these three sensory modalities are less embodied than touch and taste. A more recent study by Zhao and Huang (2018) assumed that visual, auditory, and olfactory modalities could also be differentiated in terms of the degree of embodiment, where vision and hearing should be more embodied than smell given their greater dominance in the human perceptual system. The embodiment account of linguistic synaesthesia would then predict that Mandarin visual and auditory adjectives could be used for smell, but not for touch and taste, and that Mandarin olfactory adjectives would be the least likely to transfer to other senses.

It should be noted that the embodiment account does not determine the degrees of embodiment between vision and hearing. However, the biological association account of linguistic synaesthesia proposed that synaesthetic transfers between vision and hearing are grounded in neural connections in the brain (Marks et al. 1987; Ward et al. 2006). Therefore, based on the biological association model, synaesthetic mappings from vision to hearing and from hearing to vision would both be expected in Mandarin sensory adjectives.

In what follows, the first three sections will present the synaesthetic patterns of Mandarin visual, auditory, and olfactory adjectives respectively. Based on the tendencies of Mandarin synaesthesia concerning tactile, gustatory, visual, auditory, and olfactory adjectives, a general transfer hierarchy of Mandarin synaesthesia will

Q. Zhao, *Embodied Conceptualization or Neural Realization*,
Frontiers in Chinese Linguistics 10, https://doi.org/10.1007/978-981-32-9315-1_5

be established. Section 5.4 will explore the embodiment rankings of five sensory modalities, in accordance with the tendencies of Mandarin synaesthesia.

5.1 Visual Adjectives

There are 99 Mandarin visual adjectives with synaesthetic usages involving 3034 synaesthetic instances in the Sinica corpus. As elaborated in Chap. 3, this study follows Williams (1976) to term adjectives originally for visual color/light as "color" and adjectives for dimension/shape as "dimension". Mandarin visual adjectives excluding color and dimension adjectives are named "visual situation" adjectives to facilitate discussion in this study. As illustrated in Table 5.1, synaesthetic usages were found not only among Mandarin adjectives conceptualizing color and dimension, such as 暗 *an4* 'dark' and 大 *da4* 'big' respectively, but also among adjectives representing visual situation, such as 紧 *jin3* 'tense (in vision)' and 松 *song1* 'shaggy'. Williams (1976) did not take linguistic synaesthesia of adjectives for visual situation into consideration. In contrast, this study will explore the synaesthetic patterns of Mandarin adjectives in all three visual sub-types separately (For a detailed summary of the distribution of synaesthetic uses of Mandarin visual adjectives, please see Appendix C).

5.1.1 Color

There are 30 Mandarin color adjectives originally describing visual brightness or clearness (but not chromatic categories, such as 黑 *hei1* 'black' and 红 *hong2* 'red') used for other senses in the Sinica corpus, as shown in Table 5.1. Among these adjectives, 27 adjectives exhibit synaesthetic transfers to hearing, and eight to smell. The olfactory uses of Mandarin color adjectives are consistent with the prediction of the embodiment account of linguistic synaesthesia, as elaborated in

Table 5.1 Sub-types of vision for Mandarin visual synaesthetic adjectives

Visual sub-types	Numbers of adjectives	Examples
Color	30	暗 *an4* 'dark' 亮 *liang4* 'bright'
Dimension	33	大 *da4* 'big' 小 *xiao3* 'small'
Visual situation	36	紧 *jin3* 'tense (in vision)' 松 *song1* 'shaggy'

the beginning of this chapter. With respect to the auditory distributions of Mandarin color adjectives, although the biological association account of linguistic synaesthesia predicts there synaesthetic expressions, they do not contradict an embodiment account as well, as the degrees of embodiment between vision and hearing have not been differentiated in the theory.

It is interesting that the auditory uses of Mandarin color adjectives also support both the perceived similarity basis proposed by the embodiment account and the neural connection basis suggested by the biological association account for linguistic synaesthesia. As shown in (1a–b), the adjective for low clearness (i.e., 杂 *za2* 'varicolored') was employed to describe an unpleasant auditory sensation, while the adjective for high clearness (i.e., 纯净 *chun2-jing4* 'pure') was used for a pleasant perception of hearing. Hence, the two synaesthetic examples align with the perceived similarity of subjective evaluations grounding synaesthetic transfers from vision to hearing. In addition, the perceptual "intrinsic" correspondence between brightness and pitch (Marks et al. 1987: v; Ward et al. 2006) also appears in Mandarin color adjectives. That is, adjectives for low brightness were employed to conceptualize low pitch in hearing, such as 暗 *an4* 'dark' in (1c), whereas adjectives for high brightness were used to describe auditory perceptions with a high pitch, such as 亮 *liang4* 'bright' in (1d). These synaesthetic expressions are thus consistent with a biological association basis for linguistic synaesthesia.

(1) Visual color adjectives used for hearing

a. **杂 *za2***[VISION/SOURCE] **音 *yin1***[HEARING/TARGET]

varicolored sound

'the noise'

b. **纯净 *chun2-jing4***[VISION/SOURCE] 无瑕 *wu2-xia2*

pure-clean no-flaw

的 *de* **嗓音 *sang3-yin1***[HEARING/TARGET]

NOM throat-sound

'the clean and flawless voice'

c. **音色 yin1-se4**[HEARING/TARGET] [...] 闷 *men1*

sound-color [...] stuffy

暗 an4[VISION/SOURCE]

dark

'The sound is dull and dark.'

d. **高 gao1 音 yin1**[HEARING/TARGET] 则 *ze2*

high would

亮 liang4[VISION/SOURCE]

bright

'The sound with a high pitch would be bright.'

Mandarin color adjectives used for olfactory perceptions show another interesting pattern. Adjectives for low brightness or clearness (i.e., low visibility) conceptualize the low intensity of olfactory perceptions, regardless of affective contents. As illustrated in (2a–b), both 暗 *an4* 'dark' and 隐隐 *yin3-yin3* 'faint', originally conceptualizing low visibility, were employed to denote the low intensity of olfactory perceptions. However, 暗 *an4* 'dark' was used for a pleasant smell, while 隐隐 *yin3-yin3* 'faint' represented an unpleasant odor. Mandarin visual adjectives for high brightness or clearness, however, always imply that the modified olfactory perceptions are pleasant. As shown in (2c–d), both 清 *qing1* 'limpid' and 清爽 *qing1-shuang3* 'clear' were employed for fragrance. Despite these differences, the perceived similarity basis for linguistic synaesthesia could still explain the olfactory expressions of Mandarin color adjectives. That is, the correspondence between vision and smell for adjectives of low brightness or clearness lies in their perceived intensity, whereas for adjectives of high brightness or clearness it lies in their subjective evaluation.

(2) Visual color adjectives used for smell

a.

暗 *an4*[VISION/SOURCE]	**香 *xiang1***[SMELL/TARGET]
dark	fragrant
飘 *piao1*	在 *zai4*
flutter	in
霉味 *mei2-wei*	中 *zhong1*
mildew-flavor	center

'The faint fragrance is mixing with the smell of mildew.'

b.

一股 *yi1-gu3*	**霉味 *mei2-wei4***[SMELL/TARGET]
one-CL	mildew-flavor
隐隐 *yin3-yin3*[VISION/SOURCE]	浮荡 *fu2-dang4*
faint-faint	float-sway

'There floats a faint smell of mildew.'

c.

闻 *wen2*[SMELL/TARGET]	到 *dao4*
smell	get
荷花 *he2-hua1*	的 *de*
lotus-flower	GEN
清 *qing1*[VISION/SOURCE]	**香 *xiang1***[SMELL/TARGET]
limpid	fragrant

'The delicate fragrance of lotus was perceived.'

d.

清爽 *qing1-shuang3*[VISION/SOURCE]	的 *de*
limpid-bright	NOM
芳香 *fang1-xiang1*[SMELL/TARGET]	
fragrant-fragrant	

'the delicate fragrance'

It is worth noting that Mandarin color adjectives exhibit synaesthetic transfers to touch and taste, more embodied modalities, hence at odds with the embodiment account of linguistic synaesthesia. Specifically, there are four color adjectives identified with synaesthetic distributions in touch (i.e., 清 *qing1* ‘limpid’, 清爽 *qing1-shuang3* ‘clear’, 隐隐 *yin3-yin3* ‘faint’, and 爽朗 *shuang3-lang3* ‘clear’), and four color adjectives with synaesthetic usages for taste, (i.e., 清 *qing1* ‘limpid’, 清爽 *qing1-shuang3* ‘clear’, 杂 *za2* ‘varicolored’, and 清白 *qing1-bai2* ‘clear white’).

The uses of color adjectives for touch and taste all support the perceived similarity basis for synaesthetic transfers. As shown in (3), the adjective 隐隐 *yin3-yin3* ‘faint’, originally for low brightness, preserves low intensity for tactile perceptions, and the adjective 清爽 *qing1-shuang3* ‘clear’, originally for high brightness, retains positive evaluation for touch, which are similar to their synaesthetic usages for smell. In terms of the gustatory uses of Mandarin color adjectives, their interpretations are analogous to color adjectives being used for auditory sensations, which are grounded in the perceived similarity of affective evaluations. That is, color adjectives for low brightness or clearness were utilized to describe unpleasant tastes, such as 杂 *za2* ‘varicolored’ in (4a), while adjectives for high brightness or clearness were employed to characterize pleasant gustatory sensations, such as 清爽 *qing1-shuang3* ‘clear’ in (4b). Thus, although the tactile and gustatory distributions of Mandarin color adjectives are counter-examples of the embodiment account of linguistic synaesthesia due to their mapping from a less embodied source to a more embodied target, the synaesthetic expressions of these adjectives do support the perceived similarity basis for linguistic synaesthesia suggested by the theory.

(3) Visual color adjectives used for touch

a. **隐隐 *yin3-yin3***[VISION/SOURCE] **钝痛 *dun4-tong4***[TOUCH/TARGET]

faint-faint blunt-pain

‘the weak dull pain’

b. **清爽 *qing1-shuang3***[VISION/SOURCE] 的 *de*

limpid-bright NOM

徐风 *xu2-feng1*[TOUCH/TARGET]

slow-wind

‘the refreshing zephyr’

(4) Visual color adjectives used for taste

(4) Visual color adjectives used for taste

a. 那种 *na4-zhong3* […] 食物 *shi2-wu4*，着实 *zhuo2-shi2*

that-CL […] food-object indeed-indeed

令人 *ling4-ren2* 作呕 *zuo4-ou3*,

cause-people make-vomit

酸甜苦辣 *suan1-tian2-ku3-la4*[TASTE/TARGET]

sour-sweet-bitter-hot (in taste)

杂 *za2*[VISION/SOURCE] 揉 *rou3*

varicolored mix

'The food in which sourness, sweetness, bitterness, and spicy taste are mixed really makes people throw up.'

b. **清爽 *qing1-shuang3***[VISION/SOURCE] 的 *de*

limpid-bright NOM

甜 *tian2* 味 *wei4*[TASTE/TARGET]

sweet flavor

'the refreshing sweetness'

5.1.2 Dimension

The synaesthetic distributions of Mandarin dimension adjectives are analogous to those of Mandarin color adjectives.[1] Among the 33 Mandarin dimension adjectives,

[1]Williams (1976) also established the transfer direction between color and dimension for English sensory adjectives, where dimension adjectives can transfer to color, but not vice versa. This study confirms that pattern for Mandarin sensory adjectives. Mandarin color adjectives do not transfer to dimension, while dimension adjectives do appear with color uses, such as 大红 *da4 hong2* 'bright

31 were attested with synaesthetic transfers to hearing, and three to smell, which is in line with the prediction of the embodiment account. Nevertheless, tactile and gustatory usages of Mandarin dimension adjectives also appear, contrary to what the embodiment model would predict. Among the 33 Mandarin dimension adjectives with synaesthetic distributions in the Sinica corpus, three dimension adjectives exhibit the transfer from vision to touch, and six from vision to taste.

Auditory and olfactory expressions of Mandarin dimension adjectives both support the perceived similarity basis for linguistic synaesthesia. In terms of the auditory uses of Mandarin dimension adjectives, the adjectives map to different aspects of hearing, such as 高 *gao1* 'high' and 低 *di1* 'low' to pitch, and 大 *da4* 'big' and 小 *xiao3* 'small' to loudness, as shown in (5). The polarities of adjectives on the dimension scale, however, are all preserved. In other words, the adjectives on the positive side of the dimension scales were still used for the strong side of specific auditory sub-scales, such as 高 *gao1* 'high' for high pitch and 大 *da4* 'big' for loud volume. Alternatively, the adjectives on the negative side of the dimension scale were employed for the weak side of auditory sub-scales, such as 低 *di1* 'low' for low pitch and 小 *xiao3* 'small' for low volume, as illustrated in (5).

(5) Visual dimension adjectives used for hearing

声音 *sheng1-yin1*[HEARING/TARGET]	有 *you3*
sound-voice	have
高 *gao1*[VISION/SOURCE]	**低 *di1***[VISION/SOURCE]
high	low
大 *da4*[VISION/SOURCE]	**小 *xiao3***[VISION/SOURCE]
big	small

'Sounds exhibit the differences of high pitch, low pitch, high volume, and low volume.'

---

red' and 浅绿 *qian3 lv4* 'light green'. However, intra-sensory mappings are not the focus of this study, so they will not be discussed in depth.

Mandarin dimension adjectives used for olfactory perceptions also show perceived similarity of intensity between vision and smell. As shown in (6), the adjective for small size (i.e., 薄 *bao2* 'thin') conceptualizes low olfactory intensity, while the adjective for large size (i.e., 大 *da4* 'big') denotes a smell's high intensity.

(6) Visual dimension adjectives used for smell

a.	**狐臭 *hu2-chou4***[SMELL/TARGET]		[...]
	fox-stink		[...]
	味道 *wei4-dao*[SMELL/TARGET]	[...]	**薄 *bao2***[VISION/SOURCE]
	flavor-path	[...]	thin
	'The bromhidrosis is weak.'		
b.	**体臭 *ti3-chou4***[SMELL/TARGET]		[...]
	body-stink		[...]
	味道 *wei4-dao*[SMELL/TARGET]	[...]	**大 *da4***[VISION/SOURCE]
	flavor-path	[...]	big
	'The body odor is strong.'		

Mandarin dimension adjectives with synaesthetic distributions in the Sinica corpus for touch are 细 *xi4* 'thin', 沉 *chen2* 'deep', and 薄 *bao2* 'thin'. These three dimension adjectives were used to conceptualize tactile perceptions that can be experienced typically by grasping, such as 细 *xi4* 'thin', employed to characterize the tender texture of meat in (7). Thus, the neural association between grasping-based tactile sensations and visual dimension sensations has been realized not only in Mandarin tactile adjectives (see Chap. 3), but also in Mandarin visual adjectives. Specifically, Mandarin tactile adjectives exhibit the transfer direction from touch to vision, while visual dimension adjectives demonstrate the transfer direction from vison to touch. Despite the difference of directions, both kinds of transfers suggest a biological association basis for linguistic synaesthesia, as assumed by the biological association account.

(7) Visual dimension adjectives used for touch

<u>肉质 *rou4-zhi4*</u>[TOUCH/TARGET]	**<u>细 *xi4*</u>**[VISION/SOURCE]
meat-quality	thin

'The meat is tender.'

The gustatory uses of Mandarin dimension adjectives are analogous to the auditory uses of these adjectives, with respect to their interpretations. As shown in (8), the adjective for big dimension (i.e., 厚 *hou4* 'thick') conceptualizes strong gustatory intensity, while the adjective for small dimension (i.e., 薄 *bao2* 'thin') denotes weak perceptual intensity in taste. Thus, taste retains the polarity of dimension adjectives on the dimension scale, hence supporting the perceived similarity basis for linguistic synaesthesia.

(8) Visual dimension adjectives used for taste

<u>酒 *jiu3*</u>[TASTE/TARGET]	的 *de*	**<u>厚 *hou4*</u>**[VISION/SOURCE]
wine	NOM	thick

<u>薄 *bao2*</u>[VISION/SOURCE]

thin

'the strong and weak tastes of wine'

5.1.3 Visual Situation

Mandarin adjectives for visual situation were used for hearing, smell, and touch, but not for taste in the Sinica corpus. The auditory and olfactory distributions of visual situation adjectives support the embodiment account of linguistic synaesthesia, while the tactile distribution runs contrary to the theory, as touch is assumed to be more embodied than vision (Shen 1997; Popova 2005).

There are 29 Mandarin visual situation adjectives with auditory distributions, indicating two kinds of underlying mechanisms for linguistic synaesthesia.

Specifically, some Mandarin visual situation adjectives tend to be grounded in the perceived similarity of affective evaluations. As shown in (9a), the adjective 亮丽 *liang4-li4* 'beautiful' for a positive visual sensation was employed to characterize a pleasant auditory perception, where the correspondence concerning affective evaluation between vision and hearing could be determined. Other visual situation adjectives, however, demonstrate the sensory integration basis for linguistic synaesthesia. As illustrated in (9b), the adjective 稚嫩 *zhi4-nen4* 'young (in vision)', originally conceptualizing the visual puerile sensation of children, generally describe the voice of children, where the visual property and the auditory property conceptualized by the adjective are recurrent associating characteristics of children. Thus, this kind of synaesthetic expression would suggest that sensory integration underlies these synaesthetic transfers, as they use the concept of one sensory property to describe another frequently associated sensory property.

(9) Visual situation adjectives used for hearing

a.	**音色 *yin1-se4***[HEARING/TARGET]	[…]
	sound-color	[…]
	亮丽 *liang4-li4*[VISION/SOURCE]	
	beautiful	
	'The sound is beautiful.'	
b.	**稚嫩 *zhi4-nen4***[VISION/SOURCE]	的 *de*
	young (in vision)	NOM
	童声 *tong2-sheng1*[HEARING/TARGET]	
	child-sound	
	'the young voice of children'	

Two Mandarin visual situation adjectives with olfactory uses are 清幽 *qing1-you1* 'graceful' and 细致 *xi4-zhi4* 'exquisite', both of which preserve their positive evaluations when used to describe olfactory sensations. As shown in (10), 清幽 *qing1-you1* 'graceful' for a pleasant sensation of visual situation was employed to characterize bodily fragrance. This usage thus supports the perceived similarity basis for synaesthetic transfers.

(10) Visual situation adjectives used for smell

清幽 *qing1-you1*[VISION/SOURCE]	的 *de*
graceful	NOM
体香 *ti3-xiang1*[SMELL/TARGET]	
body-fragrance	

'the graceful fragrance of the body'

There are 11 Mandarin visual situation adjectives used for touch whose interpretations are consistent with the sensory integration basis for linguistic synaesthesia. Based on behavioral and neural studies, touch and vision exhibit predominant associations, such as touching generally involving seeing behaviorally, and tactile tasks recruiting overlapping cortical regions with visual tasks (see Winter 2016a). Thus, it is not surprising that conceptualization of tactile perceptions in terms of visual concepts has been realized in language. Example (11) illustrates sensory integration between vision and touch grounding synaesthetic transfers, where the adjective 嫩 *nen4* 'delicate', originally describing the visual state of newborn objects which are easily broken and damaged, was utilized to conceptualize the easily cut or chewed texture of physical objects.

(11) Visual situation adjectives used for touch

(11) Visual situation adjectives used for touch

肉 *rou4*[TOUCH/TARGET]	**嫩 *nen4***[VISION/SOURCE]
meat	delicate
味 *wei4*	美 *mei3*
flavor	tasty

'The meat is tender, and the flavor is delicious.'

5.1.4 Synaesthetic Tendencies of Mandarin Visual Adjectives

The general synaesthetic tendencies of Mandarin visual adjectives can be determined when the synaesthetic patterns of the color, dimension, and visual situation adjectives are combined. In terms of synaesthetic distributions, 74.7% (74/99) of adjective types and 75.7% (2297/3034) of token examples for Mandarin visual adjectives are predicted by the embodiment account of linguistic synaesthesia, mapping from the more embodied (i.e., vision) to the less embodied (i.e., hearing and smell). Nevertheless, there are a small number of synaesthetic distributions of the adjectives, i.e., 25.3% (25/99) by type and 24.3% (737/3034) by token, that are used for more embodied sensory modalities (i.e., touch and taste). This runs contrary to the prediction of the embodiment model for linguistic synaesthesia. In addition, the auditory usages of visual adjectives are also consistent with the prediction of the biological association account of linguistic synaesthesia, suggesting a biological association basis for linguistic synaesthesia.

The interpretations of synaesthetic expressions with Mandarin visual adjectives have also suggested multiple underlying mechanisms of linguistic synaesthesia, including perceived similarity, biological association, and sensory integration, hence analogous to those of Mandarin tactile adjectives (see Chap. 3) and Mandarin gustatory adjectives (see Chap. 4).

5.1.5 Directionality among Touch, Taste, and Vision

The directionality of Mandarin synaesthesia between vision and touch and between vision and taste can also be established, based on both the frequency of synaesthetic transfers and the percentage of synaesthetic lexical types. With respect to the directional tendency between vision and touch for Mandarin synaesthesia, the frequency of synaesthetic transfers from touch to vision (1722 token instances) is much higher than that from vision to touch (673 token instances) in the Sinica corpus. In addition, the percentage of touch-for-vision adjectives, 84.9% (62/73), is also much higher than that of vision-for-touch adjectives with 18.2% (18/99) in Mandarin. Thus, Mandarin synaesthesia may display a tendency-based (but not absolute) directionality from touch to vision.

The directional tendency between taste and vision is similar to the one between touch and vision. That is, the synaesthetic transfers from taste to vision are much more frequent than from vision to taste in the Sinica corpus, with 1931 and 64 token examples respectively. In addition, the percentage of the taste-for-vision adjectives, 57.1% (12/21), is also much higher than the percentage of vision-for taste adjectives, which is 10.1% (10/99). Thus, the directionality from taste to vision is also tendency-based, rather than unidirectional in Mandarin synaesthesia.

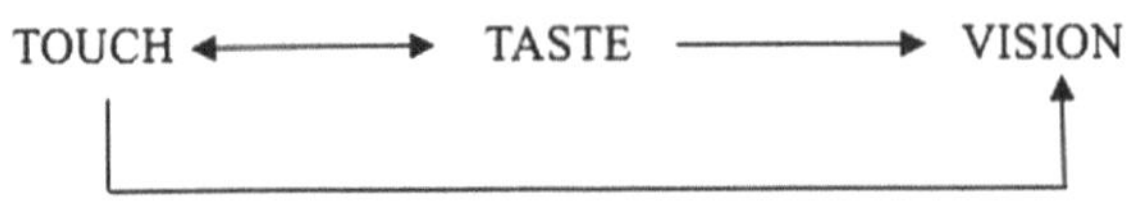

Fig. 5.1 Directional tendencies among touch, taste, and vision in Mandarin synaesthesia

The directional hierarchy of Mandarin synaesthesia containing touch, taste, and vision is summarized in Fig. 5.1, by extending Fig. 4.1 for the directionality between touch and taste (see Chap. 4).

5.2 Auditory Adjectives

There are only four Mandarin auditory adjectives identified with synaesthetic uses in the Sinica corpus: 和谐 he2-xie2 'harmonious', 喧闹 xuan1-nao4 'noisy', 吵 chao3 'loud', and 喧哗 xuan1-hua2 'noisy'. This section focuses on the synaesthetic distributions and underlying mechanisms of linguistic synaesthesia of these four Mandarin auditory adjectives. Based on the synaesthetic tendencies of Mandarin auditory adjectives, a transfer hierarchy containing touch, taste, vision, and hearing will be generalized for Mandarin synaesthesia.

5.2.1 Synaesthetic Tendencies of Mandarin Auditory Adjectives

All four Mandarin auditory synaesthetic adjectives have only visual distributions in linguistic synaesthesia. In addition, with the exception of 和谐 *he2-xie2* 'harmonious' utilized for both visual color and visual situation, the other three adjectives were employed only to characterize color in the Sinica corpus (cf. Appendix D). As mentioned at the beginning of the chapter, Mandarin auditory adjectives used for vision are predicted by both the embodiment account and the biological association account of linguistic synaesthesia.

The interpretations of Mandarin auditory adjectives used with color support both the perceived similarity basis and the biological association basis for linguistic synaesthesia. As shown in (12), the adjective 和谐 *he2-xie2* 'harmonious' describing a positive auditory sensation preserves the affective evaluation to characterize the pleasant property of color, and the adjective 喧闹 *xuan1-nao4* 'noisy' conceptualizing high loudness retains the perceptual intensity to describe an intense color. However, it should be noted that the color usage of the adjective 喧闹 *xuan1-nao4* 'noisy' is also consistent with the perceptual connection between visual brightness and auditory loudness (Marks et al. 1987; Ward et al. 2006), which indicates a neural association underlying synaesthetic transfers.

(12) Auditory adjectives used for color (vision)

a. **<u>色彩 *se4-cai3*</u>**[VISION/TARGET] **<u>和谐 *he2-xie2*</u>**[HEARING/SOURCE]

color-color harmonious

'The colors are in harmony.'

b. **<u>喧闹 *xuan1-nao4*</u>**[HEARING/SOURCE] 的 *de*

noisy NOM

<u>色彩 *se4-cai3*</u>[VISION/TARGET]

color-color

'the loud color'

The only Mandarin auditory adjective 和谐 *he2-xie2* 'harmonious,' used for visual situation, suggests a perceived similarity basis for linguistic synaesthesia. That is, the transfers from hearing to vision in the adjective preserve the positive evaluation, as shown in (13).

(13) Auditory adjectives used for visual situation (vision)

<u>画面 *hua4-mian4*</u>[VISION/TARGET] 的 *de*

painting-face NOM

<u>和谐 *he2-xie2*</u>[HEARING/SOURCE]

harmonious

'the harmony of the painting'

Fig. 5.2 Directional tendencies among touch, taste, vision, and hearing in Mandarin synaesthesia

5.2.2 Directionality among Touch, Taste, Vision, and Hearing

Mandarin tactile and gustatory adjectives were used for hearing in the Sinica corpus (see Chaps. 3 and 4), while Mandarin auditory adjectives were not attested with synaesthetic distributions in touch and taste. Thus, the directions from touch to hearing and from taste to hearing are apparent in Mandarin synaesthesia. In addition, the directionalities should be interpreted to be "absolute", as transfers in reverse directions (i.e., from hearing to touch and from hearing to taste) are not found.

Zhao and Huang (2018) generalized a bidirectionality between vision and hearing for Mandarin synaesthesia, based on the close percentages of synaesthetic lexical types for transfers from vision to hearing and from hearing to vision. This study confirms that the percentage of the vision-for-hearing adjectives is close to that of the hearing-for-vison adjectives, with 87.9% (87/99) and 100% (4/4) respectively. Nonetheless, the tendency-based directionality from vision to hearing still stands for Mandarin synaesthesia, if the frequency of synaesthetic transfers is taken into consideration. That is, synaesthetic transfers from vision to hearing exhibit a much higher frequency (2234 tokens) than the transfers from hearing to vision (30 tokens) in the Sinica corpus. The frequencies of synaesthetic transfers suggest a predominant mapping direction from vision to hearing for linguistic synaesthesia in Mandarin. Therefore, the synaesthetic directionality of touch, taste, vision, and hearing is represented in Fig. 5.2 by extending Fig. 5.1.

5.3 Olfactory Adjectives

Mandarin olfactory adjectives also occur with synaesthetic uses in the Sinica corpus (see Appendix E), which does contradict the embodiment account of linguistic synaesthesia, as smell was suggested to be the least embodied sense, and therefore least likely to map to other senses by the theory (Zhao and Huang 2018). Nevertheless, the synaesthetic distributions of Mandarin olfactory adjectives are very limited in the corpus. This section will determine the synaesthetic tendencies of Mandarin olfactory adjectives, based on which a complete transfer hierarchy for Mandarin synaesthesia can be generalized.

5.3.1 *Synaesthetic Tendencies of Mandarin Olfactory Adjectives*

There are only two Mandarin olfactory adjectives with synaesthetic uses in the Sinica corpus; one is 香 *xiang1* 'fragrant', used only with taste in 22 token examples, and the other is 臭 *chou4* 'smelly', occurring only with visual situation in ten instances. The interpretations of the synaesthetic expressions featuring these two olfactory adjectives are in line with the perceived similarity basis for synaesthetic transfers proposed by the embodiment model. As shown in (14) and (15), 香 *xiang1* 'fragrant' preserves its positive evaluation in the synaesthetic transfer from smell to taste, and 臭 *chou4* 'smelly', originally describing a negative olfactory perception, was still used to conceptualize an unpleasant sensation in vision.

(14) Olfactory adjectives used for taste

香 *xiang1*[SMELL/SOURCE]	中 *zhong1*	带 *dai4*
fragrant	center	have

涩 *se4*	的 *de*	**滋味 *zi1-wei4***[TASTE/TARGET]
rough	NOM	taste-flavor

'the fragrant taste with the astringent flavor'

(15) Olfactory adjectives used for visual situation (vision)

摆 *bai3*	出 *chu1*	一张 *yi1-zhang3*
display	out	one-CL

臭 *chou4*[SMELL/SOURCE]	**脸 *lian3***[VISION/TARGET]
smelly	face

'making an unpleasant facial expression'

5.3.2 *Directionality among Touch, Taste, Vision, Hearing, and Smell*

Before discussing the mapping directionality of the five sensory modalities, I will summarize synaesthetic transfers in Mandarin. As shown in Table 5.2, there are 20 transfer types attested in Mandarin synaesthesia among five senses, such as the mappings from touch to taste, from touch to smell, and so on, out of the 25 possible transfer types. For instance, transfers from smell to touch and from hearing to taste are not attested in the Sinica corpus for Mandarin synaesthesia.

With respect to the sub-type transfers of Mandarin synaesthesia summarized in Table 5.3, synaesthetic mappings both from hearing and from smell to other sensory modalities are limited. For example, hearing can only be used for visual color and visual situation, and smell only for gustatory quality and visual situation. Thus, both transfers among five senses and their sub-type transfers suggest that mappings of linguistic synaesthesia are not random, but instead generally conform to certain patterns. Based on Fig. 5.2 for the directional tendencies among touch, taste, vision, and hearing for Mandarin synaesthesia (see Sect. 5.2.2), a general transfer hierarchy of Mandarin synaesthesia can be postulated with the synaesthetic tendencies of smell taken into account.

Firstly, the directional tendency from touch to smell is absolute for Mandarin synaesthesia, since there are 15 Mandarin tactile adjectives used for smell with 30 synaesthetic examples, while there is no Mandarin olfactory adjective showing transfers to touch. In terms of the directionality between taste and smell, both the frequency of transfer tokens and the percentage of synaesthetic lexical types suggest a predominant direction from taste to smell for Mandarin synaesthesia. That is, the synaesthetic transfers from taste to smell (114 tokens) are more frequent than the transfers from smell to taste (22 tokens) in the Sinica corpus. In addition, the percentage of the taste-for-smell adjectives is also larger than that of the smell-for-taste adjectives, i.e., with 76.2% (16/21) and 50% (1/2) respectively.

The directional tendency between vision and smell is more complex than those between touch and smell and between taste and smell in Mandarin synaesthesia. Specifically, the frequency of synaesthetic transfers from vision to smell (63 instances) is much higher than the one from smell to vision (ten instances) in the

Table 5.2 Synaesthetic transfers between five senses of Mandarin synesthesia

Source domains	Target domains				
	TOUCH	TASTE	SMELL	VISION	HEARING
TOUCH		✓	✓	✓	✓
TASTE	✓		✓	✓	✓
SMELL		✓		✓	
VISION	✓	✓	✓		✓
HEARING				✓	

Table 5.3 A summary of sub-type transfers in Mandarin synaesthesia

Source domains		Transfer types
TOUCH	Intensity	Tactile intensity → Gustatory intensity Tactile intensity → Visual color Tactile intensity → Visual situation Tactile intensity → Hearing Tactile intensity → Smell
	Temperature	Tactile temperature → Gustatory intensity Tactile temperature → Visual color Tactile temperature → Visual situation Tactile temperature → Hearing Tactile temperature → Smell
	Hardness	Tactile hardness → Visual color Tactile hardness → Visual dimension Tactile hardness → Visual situation Tactile hardness → Hearing Tactile hardness → Smell
	Sharpness	Tactile sharpness → Visual color Tactile sharpness → Visual dimension Tactile sharpness → Visual situation Tactile sharpness → Hearing
	Dampness	Tactile dampness → Visual color Tactile dampness → Visual situation Tactile dampness → Hearing Tactile dampness → Smell
	Smoothness	Tactile smoothness → Gustatory quality Tactile smoothness → Visual dimension Tactile smoothness → Visual situation Tactile smoothness → Hearing Tactile smoothness → Smell
	Physical force	Tactile physical force → Gustatory intensity Tactile physical force → Visual color Tactile physical force → Visual situation Tactile physical force → Hearing Tactile physical force → Smell
	Pain	Tactile pain → Gustatory quality Tactile pain → Visual dimension Tactile pain → Visual situation Tactile pain → Hearing
TASTE	Intensity	Gustatory intensity → Visual color Gustatory intensity → Visual situation Gustatory intensity → Hearing Gustatory intensity → Smell
	Quality	Gustatory quality → Tactile temperature Gustatory quality → Tactile smoothness Gustatory quality → Tactile pain Gustatory quality → Visual color Gustatory quality → Visual situation Gustatory quality → Hearing Gustatory quality → Smell

(continued)

Table 5.3 (continued)

Source domains		Transfer types
VISION	Color	Visual color → Tactile intensity Visual color → Tactile pain Visual color → Gustatory intensity Visual color → Gustatory quality Visual color → Hearing Visual color → Smell
	Dimension	Visual dimension → Tactile hardness Visual dimension → Tactile physical force Visual dimension → Gustatory intensity Visual dimension → Gustatory quality Visual dimension → Hearing Visual dimension → Smell
	Visual situation	Visual situation → Tactile hardness Visual situation → Tactile physical force Visual situation → Hearing Visual situation → Smell
HEARING	Hearing	Hearing → Visual color Hearing → Visual situation
SMELL	Smell	Smell → Gustatory quality Smell → Visual situation

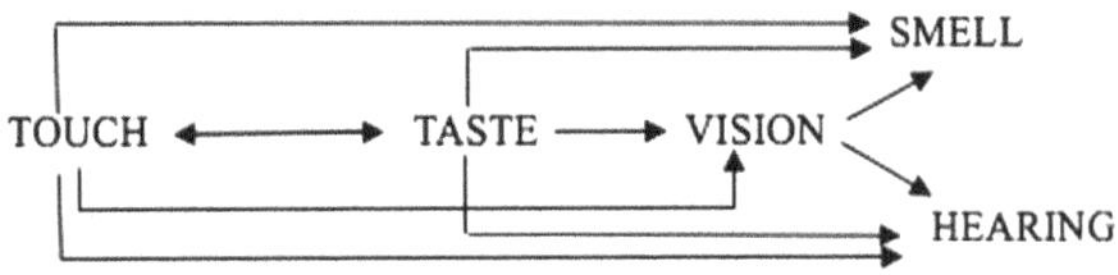

Fig. 5.3 The general transfer hierarchy of five senses in Mandarin synaesthesia

Sinica corpus. However, the percentage of vision-for-smell adjectives, 13.1% (13/99), is lower than that of the smell-for-vision adjectives, 50% (1/2). Given that synaesthetic uses of Mandarin olfactory adjectives are quite infrequent, a predominant transfer direction from vision to smell can still be generalized for Mandarin synaesthesia. In addition, the synaesthetic distributions of Mandarin olfactory adjectives in vision are also very limited, where olfactory adjectives can only be used for visual situation, not color or dimension. With respect to the directionality between hearing and smell, there is no synaesthetic transfer between these two sensory modalities attested in the Sinica corpus. Therefore, the general synaesthetic hierarchy of five senses in Mandarin Chinese appears in Fig. 5.3, an extension of the hierarchy in Fig. 5.2 (see Sect. 5.2.2).

It should be noted that Viberg (1983) found that sensory verbs showed a reverse directional tendency to sensory adjectives in languages, i.e., with the pattern vision → hearing → touch → taste/smell. Caballero and Paradis (2015) suggested that the discrepancy of hierarchies between sensory adjectives and sensory verbs resulted from the contrast between speaker-oriented and addressee-oriented perspectives. More specifically, the study proposed that the synaesthetic pattern of sensory adjectives reflected the speaker-oriented perspective, thus motivating conceptualization of less concrete and immediate sensory experiences in terms of concepts of more concrete and immediate ones. The hierarchy of sensory verbs, however, exhibit the addressee-oriented perspective, grounding the use of these concepts for more verifiable experiences to describe less verifiable ones (Caballero and Paradis 2015). It is noteworthy that linguistic synaesthesia does not occur frequently in Mandarin verbs. The Mandarin verb 闻 *wen2* 'to smell' would be the only possible case involving synaesthetic transfers, albeit a controversial one, as doubt still exists as to whether it has undergone a synaesthetic transfer from hearing to smell or just illustrates a semantic specialization from denoting both sensory activities (i.e., both hearing and smell) to conceptualizing smelling particularly in Chinese (see Hong 1989; Wang 1997; Wang and Akitani 2014; among others). Furthermore, the case, strictly speaking, does not violate the pattern in Fig. 5.3, where the directionality between hearing and smell does not occur in Mandarin sensory adjectives. Thus, it can be concluded that a synaesthetic hierarchy based on Mandarin sensory adjectives would be the most likely to describe the general transfer tendencies of Mandarin synaesthesia.

5.4 Embodiment of Five Senses

Mandarin synaesthesia does generally exhibit transfer directionality as predicted by the embodiment account of linguistic synaesthesia. Following the embodiment model, it is reasonable to assume that the directional tendencies between sensory modalities reflect the degrees of embodiment in the human senses.

Shen (1997) suggested that touch and taste are more embodied than vision, hearing, and smell, as the former two sensory modalities necessarily involve the physical contact between sensory organs and perceived objects. This is borne out in the directional tendencies of Mandarin synaesthesia. As shown by Fig. 5.3, synaesthetic directions move from touch to vision, to hearing, and to smell; and from taste to vision, to hearing, and to smell. Moreover, other linguistic evidence also suggests that touch and taste are more embodied than vision, hearing, and smell. As demonstrated in Table 2.2 in Chap. 2, more than 61% of Mandarin tactile and gustatory adjectives occur with synaesthetic uses, while less than 31% of Mandarin visual, auditory, and olfactory adjectives are identified to involve linguistic synaesthesia. Therefore, touch and taste are more frequent source domains than vision, hearing, and smell in Mandarin synaesthesia. As in the theory of Cognitive Linguistics, conceptual mappings generally map from more embodied to less embodied (see Lakoff and Johnson 1980; Gibbs 2005), touch and taste occurring more frequently as source domains in linguistic synaesthesia indicates the higher degree of embodiment of these two senses in Mandarin.

The transfer hierarchy of Mandarin synaesthesia in Fig. 5.3 suggests that both touch and taste equally are the most embodied among the five sensory modalities, as bi-directional tendencies between touch and taste appear in Mandarin synaesthesia. Thus, the embodiment ranking of touch and taste in Mandarin synaesthesia is inconsistent with Shen's (1997) assumption that touch, with sensory receptors all over the body, is more embodied than taste, which has only sensory receptors in the mouth. Nevertheless, it should be noted that it is not uncontroversial whether taste is an essentially different sense from touch or just a sub-type of touch. For instance, Popova (2005) considered taste to be a specific type of touch. In addition, the synaesthetic participation rate of Mandarin gustatory adjectives (84%) is higher than that of Mandarin tactile adjectives (61.3%) (see Table 2.2 in Sect. 2.2.2), which does not support touch having a higher degree of embodiment than taste in Mandarin either. This study will go into more detail about the cultural dominance of taste in Chinese in Chap. 7, which might motivate taste to exhibit a similar degree of embodiment to touch in Mandarin synaesthesia.

The directional tendencies of Mandarin synaesthesia also suggests the degrees of embodiment for vision, hearing, and smell. Vision is more embodied than hearing and smell, as directionality from vision to hearing and from vision to smell are both attested (see Fig. 5.3). There is other evidence to support vision having a higher degree of embodiment than hearing and smell as well. For instance, Drury et al. (1996) found that vision takes up the largest region in the brain, and Stokes and Biggs (2015) suggested that vision can influence the perceptual contents of other sensory modalities, both of which could demonstrate the dominance of vision in human perceptual systems. In addition, linguistic patters also indicate the perceptual dominance of vision. For example, Winter (2016a) found that vision has the most differential lexicalized items in English. Similarly, the visual modality has also been shown to involve the most sensory adjectives in Mandarin (664 adjectives, see Table 2.2 in Sect. 2.2.2) by this study. Based on this evidence, vision is the most embodied among the sensory modalities without physical contact between sensory organs and perceived objects.

Zhao and Huang (2018) and Zhao et al. (2018) both assumed that the lexical gap in the sensory adjectives for perceptual intensity in smell in Mandarin suggests the lowest degree of embodiment for the olfactory sense. While there are lexicalized adjectives originally conceptualizing tactile, gustatory, visual, and auditory intensities in Mandarin, such as 强 *qiang2* 'strong', 淡 *dan4* 'of mild taste', 亮 *liang4* 'bright', and 响 *xiang3* 'loud', lexicalized adjectives originally denoting olfactory intensity have not been found in Mandarin. For the ten olfactory adjectives collected for Mandarin (see Table 2.2 in Sect. 2.2.2), this study verified the assumption of Zhao and Huang (2018) and Zhao et al. (2018c). The perceptual intensity is measured exactly by the body proper. Therefore, the absence of lexicalization for olfactory intensity in Mandarin would most likely suggest the lowest body involvement (hence the lowest embodiment) in the olfactory sense among the five senses.

The directional tendencies of Mandarin synaesthesia would thus suggest that the five senses exhibit different degrees of embodiment. That is, touch and taste are the most embodied, vision follows, and hearing is less embodied, while smell is the least embodied in Mandarin. As elaborated above, the embodiment ranking of the five sensory modalities is consistent with various physiological and linguistic facts. As physiologically-based experiences can also be differentiated in terms of different degrees of embodiment, it is necessary to enrich the embodiment theory as it currently focuses on the dichotomy between embodied and non-embodied experiences in linguistic research, as noted by Caballero and Paradis (2015) and Zhao et al. (2018c). Furthermore, CMT would also call for a closer examination, as it generally employs the embodiment theory to explore metaphors (see Sect. 1.1.3), and linguistic synaesthesia can be analyzed as a kind of metaphor. Chap. 7 will return to these two theoretical issues. The next chapter will provide another piece of evidence to support the embodiment rankings of the five senses in Mandarin Chinese by focusing on the synaesthetic tendencies of Mandarin compound adjectives that combine different sensory modalities.

References

Caballero, Rosario, and Carita Paradis. 2015. Making sense of sensory perceptions across languages and cultures. *Functions of Language* 22 (1): 1–19.

Drury, Heather A., David C. Van Essen, Charles H. Anderson, Chris W. Lee, Thomas A. Coogan, and James W. Lewis. 1996. Computerized mappings of the cerebral cortex: A multiresolution flattening method and a surface-based coordinate system. *Journal of Cognitive Neuroscience* 8: 1–28.

Gibbs, Raymond W. 2005. *Embodiment and cognitive science*. New York: Cambridge University Press.

Hong, Chengyu (洪成玉). 1989. A study on wen2 [释 "闻"]. *Beijing Normal College (Social Science Edition)* [北京师范学院学报(社会科学版)] 5: 107–112.

Lakoff, George, and Mark Johnson. 1980. *Metaphors we live by*. Chicago: University of Chicago Press.

Marks, Lawrence, Robin Hammeal, Marc Bornstein, and Linda Smith. 1987. Perceiving similarity and comprehending metaphor. *Monographs of the Society for Research in Child Development* 52 (1): 1–100.

Popova, Yanna. 2005. Image schemas and verbal synaesthesia. In *From perception to meaning: Image schema in cognitive linguistics (cognitive linguistics research 29)*, ed. Beate Hampe and Joseph Grady, 395–420. Berlin and New York: Mouton de Gruyter.

Shen, Yeshayahu. 1997. Cognitive constraints on poetic figures. *Cognitive Linguistics* 8 (1): 33–71.

Stokes, Dustin, and Stephen Biggs. 2015. The dominance of the visual. In *Perception and its modalities*, ed. Stokes Dustin, M. Matthen, and Stephen Biggs, 350–378. Oxford: Oxford University Press.

Viberg, Åke. 1983. The verbs of perception: A typological study. *Linguistics* 21 (1): 123–162.

Wang, Weihui (汪维辉) and Hiroyuki Akitani (秋谷裕幸). 2014. Synchronic distribution and diachronic development of words encoding "to smell" in Chinese [汉语"闻/嗅"义词的现状与历史]. *Language and Linguistics* [语言暨语言学] 15(5): 699–732.

Wang, Ying (王锳). 1997. The meaning extension based on synaesthesia: A case study on wen2 [试论"通感生义"——从"闻"字说起]. *Language Teaching and Linguistic Studies* [语言教学与研究] 4: 23–28.

Ward, Jamie, Brett Huckstep, and Elias Tsakanikos. 2006. Sound-colour synaesthesia: To what extent does it use cross-modal mechanisms common to us all? *Cortex* 42 (2): 264–280.

Williams, Joseph. 1976. Synaesthetic adjectives: A possible law of sematic change. *Language* 52 (2): 461–478.

Winter, Bodo. 2016a. *The sensory structure of the English lexicon*. Merced, CA: University of California, Merced dissertation.

Zhao, Qingqing (赵青青) and Chu-Ren Huang (黄居仁). 2018. Mapping models and underlying mechanisms of synaesthetic metaphors in Mandarin [现代汉语通感隐喻的映射模型与制约机制]. *Language Teaching and Linguistic Studies* [语言教学与研究] 1: 44–55.

Zhao, Qingqing, Chu-Ren Huang, and Yat-mei Sophia Lee. 2018c. From linguistic synaesthesia to embodiment: Asymmetrical representations of taste and smell in Mandarin Chinese. In *Chinese lexical semantics (LNAI 10709)*, ed. Yunfang Wu, Jia Fei Hong, and Qi Su, 406–413. Gewerbestrasse: Springer International Publishing.

Chapter 6
Mandarin Compound Adjectives Combining Different Modalities

Zhao and Huang (2018) demonstrated that compound Mandarin sensory adjectives comprised of two concepts originally for different senses also followed the directionality tendencies of linguistic synaesthesia. The transfer directions of these adjectives are consistent with the directions of the constituent morpheme in each compound that represents a higher sensory modality on the transfer hierarchy of linguistic synaesthesia (Zhao and Huang 2018). For instance, Zhao and Huang (2018) found that compound adjectives that combine taste and vision, such as 醇厚 *chun2-hou4* 'mellow' (taste + vision) and 清淡 *qing1-dan4* 'light' (vision + taste), had synaesthetic distributions in hearing and smell, but not in touch, such as 醇厚歌声 *chun2-hou4 ge1-sheng1* 'the mellow singing' and 清淡的荷花香气 *qing1-dan4 de he2-hua1 xiang1-qi4* 'the slight fragrance of the lotus'. Thus, the adjectives combining taste and vision shared the same synaesthetic distributions as the constituent morpheme conceptualizing vision, which occupies a higher position than taste on the hierarchy for Mandarin synaesthesia, with tendency-based mappings to hearing and smell, but not to touch (Zhao and Huang 2018).

This chapter will employ a much larger data sample to test Zhao and Huang's (2018) assumption. Sixty-one adjectives and 538 synaesthetic instances were extracted from the Sinica corpus. This chapter will examine the validity of the embodiment rankings of the five sensory modalities discussed in the last chapter (see Sect. 5.4) for Mandarin compound adjectives combining different senses in linguistic synaesthesia. Specifically, Sect. 6.1 will focus on the general synaesthetic tendencies of Mandarin compound adjectives containing morphemes based in different senses. Section 6.2 will discuss compound adjectives that combine any two of the three sensory modalities including touch, taste, and vision, as these adjectives frequently occur in linguistic synaesthetic expressions. The last section will compare the synaesthetic patterns of Mandarin compound adjectives with different sensory modalities to the patterns of Mandarin adjectives involving a single sensory modality (i.e., Mandarin tactile, gustatory, visual, auditory, and olfactory adjectives elaborated in the last three chapters).

Q. Zhao, *Embodied Conceptualization or Neural Realization*,
Frontiers in Chinese Linguistics 10, https://doi.org/10.1007/978-981-32-9315-1_6

6.1 Synaesthetic Patterns

The transfer hierarchy of Mandarin synaesthesia depicted in Fig. 5.3 has shown that hearing and smell share the highest position on the hierarchy, and that these two sensory modalities occur infrequently as source domains for synaesthetic mappings (see Sect. 5.3.2). Given Zhao and Huang's (2018) claim that compound adjectives combining different senses shared the same synaesthetic distributions as their constituent morphemes conceptualizing a higher sense on the synaesthetic hierarchy, one could predict that Mandarin compound adjectives combining either hearing or smell are the least frequent to have synaesthetic distributions.

Table 6.1 shows that the synaesthetic data for Mandarin compound adjectives with different sensory modalities in the Sinica corpus supports Zhao and Huang's (2018) assumption. Specifically, if disregarding the combination order of senses, there are six combination patterns for the compound adjectives. Among these adjectives, the ones combining touch and hearing (e.g., 柔和 *rou2-he2* 'soft'), touch and smell (e.g., 温馨 *wen1-xin1* 'cozy'), and hearing and taste (e.g., 平淡 *ping2-dan4* 'dull') all occupy very small percentages. The percentages of lexical types are all smaller than 5% and the percentages of token examples are all less than 16%. In terms of the cumulative percentages of the compound adjectives with these three combination patterns, the lexical types occupy 8.2% (5/61), and the token examples represent 22.7% (122/538). Thus, as predicted by Zhao and Huang (2018), linguistic synaesthesia was not frequent in Mandarin compound adjectives composed of different senses related to hearing or smell.

Linguistic synaesthesia has, however, been attested frequently in Mandarin compound adjectives combining touch and vision (e.g., 粗壮 *cu1-zhuang4* 'burly'),

Table 6.1 Data distributions of synaesthetic uses of Mandarin compound adjectives combining different sensory modalities

Compound patterns	Type percentages	Token percentages	Examples of adjectives
TOUCH + VISION VISION + TOUCH	55.8% (34/61)	39.9% (215/538)	粗壮 *cu1-zhuang4* 'burly'
TOUCH + TASTE TASTE + TOUCH	21.3% (13/61)	27.9% (150/538)	苦涩 *ku3-se4* 'bitter'
TASTE + VISION VISION + TASTE	14.8% (9/61)	9.5% (51/538)	清淡 *qing1-dan4* 'light'
TOUCH + HEARING HEARING + TOUCH	**4.9% (3/61)**	**15.2% (82/538)**	柔和 ***rou2-he2* 'soft'**
TOUCH + SMELL	**1.6% (1/61)**	**7.1% (38/538)**	温馨 ***wen1-xin1* 'cozy'**
HEARING + TASTE	**1.6% (1/61)**	**0.4% (2/538)**	平淡 ***ping2-dan4* 'dull'**
Total	100% (61/61)	100% (538/538)	–

touch and taste (e.g., 苦涩 *ku3-se4* ‘bitter’), and taste and vision (e.g., 清淡 *qing1-dan4* ‘light’). The cumulative percentages of these three types of adjectives are 91.8% (56/61) by lexical type and 77.3% (416/538) by lexical token among all synaesthetic compound adjectives, as shown in Table 6.1. As touch, taste, and vision are not on the highest position in the hierarchy of Mandarin synaesthesia (see Fig. 5.3), and these three senses display synaesthetic transfers, the frequent synaesthetic usages of Mandarin compound adjectives combining any two of these three modalities could support Zhao and Huang’s (2018) theory. In addition, among touch, taste, and vision, vision is the sensory modality on a higher position in the transfer hierarchy of Mandarin synaesthesia, and vision can have synaesthetic mappings to hearing and smell (see Sect. 5.1). Thus, following Zhao and Huang’s (2018) theory, Mandarin compound adjectives combining any two senses from touch, taste, and vision would at least have synaesthetic distributions in hearing and smell. I will return to this hypothesis through examining the synaesthetic distributions of these adjectives in the next section. First, it is necessary to have a look at the interpretations of the synaesthetic uses of compound adjectives combining different sensory modalities.

Examples (1) through (6) illustrate the synaesthetic usages of these Mandarin compound adjectives. All these examples support the perceived similarity basis for linguistic synaesthesia, as suggested by the embodiment account.

Specifically, as shown in (1a), the adjective 轻微 *qing1-wei1* ‘slight’, combining morphemes originally for tactile perception and visual perception, both with weak perceptual intensity, characterizes an auditory sensation with weak intensity. Similarly, the adjective 细滑 *xi4-hua2* ‘fine and smooth’, containing the concept for a neutral visual sensation with a positive tactile sensation (i.e., smoothness), was used to describe a fragrance with a pleasant odor, as in (1b). Thus, the synaesthetic uses of the compound adjectives combining touch and vision support a perceived similarity basis for linguistic synaesthesia, as they retains their intensity pole or subjective evaluation when applied to a new sensory domain.

(1) a. **轻微 *qing1-wei1***$_{[(\text{TOUCH + VISION})/\text{SOURCE}]}$ 的 *de*

light (in weight)-small NOM

声音 *sheng1-yin1*$_{[\text{HEARING/TARGET}]}$

sound-voice

‘the slight sound’

b. <u>***香气 xiang1-qi4***</u>[SMELL/TARGET] [...]

fragrant-air

<u>***细滑 xi4-hua2***</u>[(VISION + TOUCH)/SOURCE]

thin-smooth

'The fragrance is light and smooth.'

The synaesthetic usages of Mandarin compound adjectives combining touch and taste are also consistent with the perceived similarity basis, where the correspondences between source and target sensory modalities are concerned with perceptual intensity or affective evaluation. As shown in (2a), the adjective 浓烈 *nong2-lie4* 'strong', with constituent morphemes both related to a strong perceptual intensity, was utilized for a strong perceptual intensity related to smell. The adjective 柔美 *rou2-mei3* 'graceful' in (2b) characterizes a pleasant sensation related to hearing, whose constituent morphemes conceptualize a positive tactile sensation and a positive gustatory perception respectively.

(2) a. <u>***浓烈 nong2-lie4***</u>[(TASTE + TOUCH)/SOURCE] [...]

of intense taste-scorching

<u>***油漆味 you2-qi1-wei4***</u>[SMELL/TARGET]

oil-paint-flavor

'the strong smell of the oil paint'

b. <u>***柔美 rou2-mei3***</u>[(TOUCH + TASTE)/SOURCE] 的 *de*

soft-tasty NOM

<u>***声音 sheng1-yin1***</u>[HEARING/TARGET]

sound-voice

'the soft and pleasant sound'

The adjective 浓郁 *nong2-yu4* 'strong', combining a strong taste and a strong visual sensation in (3a), also shows that the perceived similarity of perceptual intensity can ground synaesthetic transfers, as the adjective preserves its positive pole on the perceptual intensity scale when used for smelling. Example (3b) illustrates the perceived similarity of affective evaluation for linguistic synaesthesia, where 清甜 *qing1-tian2* 'slightly sweet', combining a positive visual perception and a positive gustatory perception, was employed to characterize the pleasant odor of rice.

a. **浓郁 *nong2-yu4***[(TASTE + VISION)/SOURCE] 的 *de*

of intense taste-dense NOM

血腥味 *xue3-xing1-wei4*[SMELL/TARGET]

blood-of fishy smell-flavor

'the strong smell of blood'

b. **清甜 *qing1-tian2***[(VISION + TASTE)/SOURCE] 的 *de*

limpid-sweet NOM

米香 *mi3-xiang1*[SMELL/TARGET]

rice-fragrance

'the slightly sweet fragrance of rice'

Mandarin compound adjectives combining touch and hearing, and touch and smell, both support the perceived similarity of subjective evaluation in linguistic synaesthesia. As shown in (4), the adjective 柔和 *rou2-he2* 'soft', comprising a positive tactile sensation and a positive auditory sensation, occurred with a pleasant sensation of vision. Similarly, the adjective 温馨 *wen1-xin1* 'cozy', combining a pleasant temperature and a pleasant smell, describes the positive visual sensation in (5). The adjective 平淡 *ping2-dan4* 'dull' combining hearing and taste, both of which feature weak perceptual intensity, conceptualizes the weak visual intensity of color sensations in (6). Thus, the expression also demonstrates the perceived similarity of perceptual intensity underlying linguistic synaesthesia.

(4) **柔和 *rou2-he2***[(TOUCH + HEARING)/SOURCE] 的 *de*

soft-harmonious NOM

灯光 *deng1-guang1*[VISION/TARGET]

lamp-light

'the soft lamplight'

(5) **画面 *hua4-mian4***[VISION/TARGET]

painting-face

温馨 *wen1-xin1*[(TOUCH + SMELL)/SOURCE]

lukewarm-fragrant

'The painting looks cozy.'

(6) **色彩 *se4-cai3***[VISION/TARGET] **平淡 *ping2-dan4***[(VISION + TASTE)/SOURCE]

color-color of level tone-of mild taste

'The color is dull.'

To summarize, linguistic synaesthesia does not frequently occur in Mandarin compound adjectives that combine senses related to hearing or smell. However, synaesthetic usages of Mandarin compound adjectives combining two senses from touch, taste, and vision occur frequently. Thus, synaesthetic distributions of compound adjectives with different sensory modalities are consistent with the predictions of Zhao and Huang (2018). With respect to the interpretations, the synaesthetic uses of these compound adjectives support a perceived similarity basis for linguistic synaesthesia.

6.2 Compound Adjectives Combining Touch, Taste, and Vision

Mandarin compound adjectives combining any two of touch, taste, and vision are employed frequently in linguistic synaesthesia, and vision occupies a higher position than touch and taste on the transfer hierarchy of Mandarin synaesthesia. Zhao and Huang (2018) claimed that Mandarin compound adjectives combining different senses shared the same synaesthetic distributions with constituent morpheme representing the sense that holds a higher position on the synaesthetic hierarchy. This section will test their claim based on further empirical data from the Sinica corpus.

Mandarin compound adjectives combining touch and vision occur with synaesthetic distributions in hearing, smell, and taste, as shown in Table 6.2. The auditory and olfactory uses of these adjectives are consistent with the prediction of Zhao and Huang (2018), where vision is on a higher position than touch in the synaesthetic hierarchy with transfer directions to hearing and smell. Contrary to expectation, Zhao and Huang (2018) did not predict the gustatory uses of these adjectives since the higher constituent modality (i.e., vision) was not expected to map to taste in Mandarin synaesthesia. It is important, to note, however, that the gustatory distributions of compound adjectives are quite infrequent, with only 5.9% (2/34) by lexical type and 2.3% (5/215) by lexical token. Moreover, vision also occurs infrequently in synaesthetic transfers to taste (see Chap. 5). Thus, the general

Table 6.2 Synaesthetic distributions of Mandarin compound adjectives combining touch, taste, and vision

Source domains	Target domains		
TOUCH + VISION VISION + TOUCH	HEARING	SMELL	**TASTE**
Transferability of adjectives	91.2% (31/34)	17.6% (6/34)	**5.9% (2/34)**
Percentage of synaesthetic tokens	94.9% (204/215)	2.8% (6/215)	**2.3% (5/215)**
TOUCH + TASTE TASTE + TOUCH	VISION	HEARING	SMELL
Transferability of adjectives	84.6% (11/13)	61.5% (8/13)	38.5% (5/13)
Percentage of synaesthetic tokens	60% (90/150)	28% (42/150)	12% (18/150)
TASTE + VISION VISION + TASTE	HEARING	SMELL	**TOUCH**
Transferability of adjectives	44.4% (4/9)	66.7% (6/9)	**11.1% (1/9)**
Percentage of synaesthetic tokens	27.5% (14/51)	68.6% (35/51)	**3.9% (2/51)**

synaesthetic distributions of Mandarin compound adjectives combining touch and vision show a tendency-based (but not absolute) synaesthetic directionality, analogous to the distributions of the adjectives consisting of only the visual modality in Mandarin synaesthesia. Therefore, these distributions verify the assumption of Zhao and Huang (2018).

If distributions follow the prediction of Zhao and Huang (2018), Mandarin compound adjectives combining touch and taste should have distributions in vision, hearing, and smell, as touch and taste are both on the lowest position in the transfer hierarchy of Mandarin synaesthesia. As demonstrated in Table 6.2, the visual, auditory, and olfactory usages of the Mandarin compound adjectives combining touch and taste have all been found in the Sinica corpus, hence confirming Zhao and Huang's (2018) hypothesis.

The synaesthetic pattern of Mandarin compound adjectives combining taste and vision is analogous to the pattern of Mandarin compound adjectives combining touch and vision discussed above. That is, counter-examples to the prediction of Zhao and Huang (2018), i.e., tactile usages of the compound adjectives combining taste and vision, exist. The exceptions, however, occupy quite small proportions, with 11.1% (1/9) in terms of lexical types and 3.9% (2/51) in terms of token examples. Therefore, Mandarin compound adjectives combining taste and vision also exhibit a tendency-based synaesthetic directionality with transfers to hearing and smell, as predicted by Zhao and Huang (2018).

It can thus be concluded that the distributions of the synaesthetic uses of Mandarin compound adjectives combining touch and vision, touch and taste, and taste and vision in the Sinica corpus confirm Zhao and Huang's (2018) assumption: The adjectives share the same tendency-based mapping directionalities with their constituent sensory modalities that occupy a higher position in the Mandarin synaesthesia transfer hierarchy.

6.3 Comparisons with Adjectives Involving One Modality

Mandarin compound adjectives combining different senses share both similarities and differences with adjectives involving only one sensory modality in Mandarin synaesthesia (see Chaps. 3 through 5).

Specifically, both compound adjectives combining different senses and adjectives involving one sense follow mapping directionalities in Mandarin synaesthesia, and these directionalities are tendency-based rather than absolute. In addition, the interpretations of the synaesthetic usages of both kinds of adjectives support a perceived similarity basis for linguistic synaesthesia suggested by the embodiment account.

The differences between compound adjectives combining different senses and adjectives involving one sense are as follows: (1) compound adjectives follow the directional tendencies of the constituent modality on a higher position in the synaesthetic hierarchy, while adjectives involving one sense do not exhibit this pattern when constituent modalities share the same position on the synaesthetic hierarchy; and (2) synaesthetic uses of compound adjectives suggest only a perceived similarity basis for linguistic synaesthesia, whereas synaesthetic uses of adjectives involving one sense demonstrate three possible mechanisms underlying linguistic synaesthesia, including perceived similarity, sensory integration, and biological association.

It is intriguing that both the similarities and differences between these adjective types can be explained by the embodiment degrees of sensory modalities. With respect to the similarities, the directional tendencies of both kinds of adjectives are consistent with the different degrees of embodiment in the human senses, which motivate synaesthetic mappings from a more embodied source to a less embodied target. In addition, the perceived similarity basis for linguistic synaesthesia suggested by both compound adjectives combining different senses and the adjectives involving one sense in Mandarin synaesthesia also highlights the role of bodily experiences in structuring language, as proposed by the embodiment account of linguistic synaesthesia (Shen 1997; Popova 2005).

The differences between the compound adjectives combining different senses and the adjectives involving one sense in Mandarin synaesthesia can be predicted by the embodiment ranking of the five senses, which is touch/taste > vision > hearing > smell (see Chap. 5). Specifically, one can expect that compound adjectives combining different senses show the same directional tendencies as the constituent sense that occupies a higher position in the synaesthetic hierarchy, when considering that the constituent senses have different degrees of embodiment and that the sense in the higher position is less embodied. In addition, as hearing and smell are the least embodied, Mandarin compound adjectives containing either hearing or smell having infrequent synaesthetic distributions would make sense. Similarly, compound adjectives combining any two of the senses of touch, taste, and vision are used frequently in linguistic synaesthesia for hearing and smell, which is consistent with the theory that touch, taste, and vision are more embodied that hearing and smell. With respect to the differences in the underlying mechanisms for linguistic synaesthesia, compound adjectives combining different senses are more constrained than adjectives involving one sensory modality in synaesthetic usages. Thus, it can be expected that compound adjectives do not show all possible mechanisms that could underlie linguistic synaesthesia, but only demonstrate the most common one, which is a perceived similarity basis for Mandarin synaesthesia.

The next chapter will explore the theoretical implications of linguistic synaesthesia on the basis of the synaesthetic patterns of both compound adjectives combining different senses and adjectives involving one sense in Mandarin Chinese.

References

Popova, Yanna. 2005. Image schemas and verbal synaesthesia. In *From perception to meaning: Image schema in cognitive linguistics (Cognitive Linguistics Research 29)*, ed. Beate Hampe and Joseph Grady, 395–420. Berlin and New York: Mouton de Gruyter.

Shen, Yeshayahu. 1997. Cognitive constraints on poetic figures. *Cognitive Linguistics* 8(1): 33–71.

Zhao, Qingqing (赵青青) and Chu-Ren Huang (黄居仁). 2018. Mapping models and underlying mechanisms of synaesthetic metaphors in Mandarin [现代汉语通感隐喻的映射模型与制约机制]. *Language Teaching and Linguistic Studies* [语言教学与研究] 1: 44–55.

Chapter 7
From Linguistic Synaesthesia to Conceptual Metaphor Theory

This chapter aims to establish correlations between synaesthetic tendencies in Mandarin and theoretical accounts of linguistic synaesthesia. It will also clarify the nature of linguistic synaesthesia based on the synaesthetic tendencies of Mandarin sensory adjectives. Furthermore, a finer-grained account of embodiment will be suggested to refine CMT to ensure that linguistic synaesthesia can be folded into the theory.

Specifically, Sect. 7.1 will demonstrate that neither the embodiment account nor the biological association account for linguistic synaesthesia proposed in the literature can fully predict the distributions and tendencies of the synaesthetic uses of Mandarin sensory adjectives in the Sinica corpus. As the data suggest that both an embodiment mechanism and a biological mechanism underlie Mandarin synaesthesia, I will suggest an incorporated theoretical model containing both mechanisms for linguistic synaesthesia. Section 7.2 will establish that linguistic synaesthesia is unlikely to be merely a neural realization of sensory associations. Rather, I will argue for the metaphorical nature of linguistic synaesthesia arguing that linguistic synaesthesia should also be considered an embodied conceptualization similar to canonical metaphors that map from bodily experiences to non-bodily experiences. In order to analyze linguistic synaesthesia in the framework of CMT, I will propose a finer-grained account of embodiment covering the notions of degrees of embodiment and types of embodied events to enrich CMT. The last section will summarize the theoretical implications of linguistic synaesthesia from both the linguistic and inter-disciplinary perspectives.

7.1 Mandarin Synaesthesia and Theoretical Models

It has been demonstrated that theoretical models of linguistic synaesthesia differ in their assumptions of how linguistic synaesthesia is realized in the language. Specifically, the embodiment account predicts the directionality of synaesthetic

Q. Zhao, *Embodied Conceptualization or Neural Realization*,
Frontiers in Chinese Linguistics 10, https://doi.org/10.1007/978-981-32-9315-1_7

transfers from more embodied modalities to less embodied ones, and the biological association account suggests the cross-linguistic universality of synaesthetic tendencies. In addition, the embodiment account proposes that a perceived similarity of intensity and subjective evaluation grounds linguistic synaesthesia, and the biological association account assumes neural association underlying linguistic synaesthesia (see Sect. 1.1.2). Based on the tendencies of linguistic synaesthesia in Mandarin Chinese, this section will examine to what extent the proposals of these theoretical models can be supported.

7.1.1 Directionality and Perceived Similarity

Chapters 3 through 5 have shown that linguistic synaesthesia of Mandarin tactile, gustatory, visual, auditory, and olfactory adjectives do exhibit mapping directionalities, as predicted by the embodiment account. More specifically, the directional tendencies move from touch to vision, from touch to hearing, from touch to smell, from taste to vision, from taste to hearing, from taste to smell, from vision to hearing, and from vision to smell (see Fig. 5.3 in Chap. 5). In addition, Mandarin compound adjectives combining different sensory modalities also follow directionality tendencies. The adjectives share the directional patterns of the constituent sense that resides in a higher position on the transfer hierarchy (see Chap. 6).

However, two important issues should be noted with respect to directionality in Mandarin synaesthesia. First, except for synaesthetic transfers from touch to hearing, from touch to smell, and from taste to hearing, all other directional patterns are tendency-based rather than absolute, as assumed by Strik Lievers (2015). For instance, the overall agreement of Mandarin gustatory adjectives with the prediction mapping from more embodied to less embodied is 76.2% (16/21) for lexical types and 95.5% (2187/2291) for lexical tokens (See Sect. 4.3). Similarly, 74.7% (74/99) by type and 75.7% (2297/3034) by token of Mandarin visual adjectives are used for less embodied sensory modalities, i.e., hearing and smell (See Sect. 5.1.4). Moreover, the unidirectional tendency was not observed between touch and taste. Rather, linguistic synaesthesia in Mandarin Chinese exhibits bi-directional mappings from touch to taste and from taste to touch, different from Indo-European languages (e.g., Williams 1976; Strik Lievers 2015). Therefore, the embodiment model of linguistic synaesthesia predicts most but not all synaesthetic transfers of Mandarin sensory adjectives, as synaesthetic uses violating the directionality principle exist.

The other issue concerning the directionality proposal of the embodiment account relates to the synaesthetic patterns of touch and vision, both of which are multi-dimensional (Miller and Johnson-Laird 1976; Purves et al. 2001 [2000]). For instance, touch includes sensations such as temperature, hardness, and so on, and vision includes perceptions for color, dimension, and so forth. The directionality proposal of the embodiment account only considers mappings among the five sensory modalities, and thus does not predict different sub-domains of tactile and visual modalities with distinct patterns in linguistic synaesthesia. One of the most intriguing patterns is concerned with the visual sensation of dimension. Specifically, only Mandarin tactile adjectives conceptualizing tactile perceptions experienced typically by hands' grasping, such as 粗 *cu1* 'rough' and 尖 *jian1* 'sharp', have been found with synaesthetic uses for visual dimension, while Mandarin adjectives in other tactile sub-domains and in other sensory domains (including taste, hearing, and smell) do not (see Table 5.3 in Sect. 5.3.2).

The perceived similarity of intensity and subjective evaluation that underlies synaesthetic transfers as suggested by the embodiment account has also been confirmed by most Mandarin synaesthetic expressions. For instance, Mandarin adjectives originally conceptualizing perceptual intensity retain their polarity on the intensity scale in their synaesthetic uses, such as gustatory adjectives 浓 *nong2* 'of intense taste', used to represent the strong intensity in vision (e.g., 浓绿 *nong2 lv4* 'deep-green'), and 淡 *dan4* 'of mild taste', employed for weak perceptual intensity in olfactory perceptions (e.g., 淡淡的花香 *dan4-dan4 de hua1-xiang1* 'the slight fragrance of flowers'). Similarly, Mandarin adjectives for specific perceptual properties generally preserve their affective evaluation in linguistic synaesthesia. For instance, the adjective 柔 *rou2* 'soft', originally for a positive tactile perception, conceptualizes pleasant sensations in hearing (e.g., 柔声 *rou2 sheng1* 'in a soft voice'), and the adjective 冰冷 *bing1-leng3* 'ice-cold', originally for a negative tactile sensation, denotes unpleasant perceptions in vision (e.g., 冰冷的眼光 *bing1-leng3 de yan3-guang1* 'cold eye expressions'). Nevertheless, there are synaesthetic examples in Mandarin which cannot be explained by a perceived similarity basis between source and target sensory domains. Take the aforementioned synaesthetic pattern concerning visual dimension for example: In addition to Mandarin tactile adjectives conceptualizing grasping-based perceptions being found to have synaesthetic distributions in visual dimension, Mandarin visual adjectives originally characterizing visual dimension were also used for tactile perceptions which can be experienced by grasping, such as 细 *xi4* 'thin' and 薄 *bao2* 'thin'. However, among the synaesthetic transfers between tactile grasping-based sensations and visual dimension, no correspondence of perceptual intensity nor subjective evaluation could be determined between touch and vision. These bi-directional synaesthetic transfers are, nevertheless, consistent with the neural association between touch and vision in shape perceptions discovered by Amedi et al. (2002). In addition, synaesthetic expressions such as Mandarin temperature adjectives used for color (e.g., 冷 *leng3* 'cold', 暖 *nuan3* 'warm'), and gustatory adjectives originally conceptualizing unpleasant tastes (苦 *ku3* 'bitter' and 酸 *suan1* 'sour') employed for a pleasant smell, suggest a sensory integration basis for linguistic synaesthesia.

In sum, most synaesthetic uses of Mandarin sensory adjectives support the assumptions of directionality and perceived similarity in the embodiment account for linguistic synaesthesia. However, neither assumption holds for all Mandarin synaesthetic expressions. In other words, Mandarin synaesthesia only exhibits tendency-based and not absolute directionality patterns. In addition, synaesthetic transfers of Mandarin sensory adjectives can be grounded not only in perceived similarity of intensity and subjective evaluation, but also in biological association and sensory integration.

7.1.2 Universality and Biological Association

Zhao et al. (2018b) employed a corpus-based approach to investigate the synaesthetic uses of gustatory adjectives in Mandarin and English. Their study found that Mandarin and English did not share the same synaesthetic patterns, the main difference being the relative positions of vision and hearing on the synaesthetic hierarchy: Vision precedes hearing for Mandarin gustatory adjectives, while vision follows hearing for English gustatory adjectives. Additionally, Zhao and Huang's (2018) dictionary-based study also demonstrated that the general transfer hierarchy of Mandarin synaesthesia is different from that of English synaesthesia generalized by Williams (1976). For instance, the transfers between touch and taste are bi-directional in Mandarin synaesthesia but unidirectional in English synaesthesia (Zhao and Huang 2018).

This comprehensive corpus-driven research confirms the findings of Zhao et al. (2018b) and Zhao and Huang (2018). In other words, Mandarin synaesthesia shows both commonalities and differences when compared to the attested synaesthetic patterns for English. As Williams' (1976) hierarchy for English synaesthesia is compatible with but stronger than Ullmann's (1957) (see Sect. 1.1.1), I compare the general synaesthetic hierarchy for Mandarin Chinese (cf. Fig. 5.3 in Chap. 5) with the Williams' model.

Specifically, similar patterns of linguistic synaesthesia in Mandarin and English include: (1) synaesthetic transfers from touch to hearing, from taste to smell, and from taste to hearing show the same directionality in both Mandarin synaesthesia and English synaesthesia; and (2) the olfactory sense occurs only as the target domain in both Mandarin synaesthesia and English synaesthesia.

The differences in synaesthetic tendencies between Mandarin and English, however, are more intriguing, including: (1) synaesthetic directions from touch to taste and from taste to touch are both possible in Mandarin while only the direction, from touch to taste, has been attested in English; (2) touch can transfer to both color and dimension in the visual modality in Mandarin, whereas touch can only map to color in English; (3) touch has been attested with synaesthetic transfers to smell in Mandarin, but not in English; and (4) taste has been identified with synaesthetic uses for vision including color in Mandarin, while taste does not transfer to color in English. Therefore, Mandarin synaesthesia does not show the same transfer tendencies as English synaesthesia, which thus does not support the cross-linguistic universality of synaesthetic patterns assumed by the biological association account for linguistic synaesthesia.

With respect to the underlying mechanisms of linguistic synaesthesia, a biological association basis has been established for some Mandarin synaesthetic expressions. Precisely speaking, these expressions are: (1) the gustatory distribution of tactile adjective 麻 *ma2* 'trembling', which shows the shared neural channel between the sharp taste induced by a Szechuan pepper and the tactile sensation produced by mechanical vibration; (2) the tactile use of the gustatory adjective 辣 *la4* 'hot (in taste)', which indicates the neural associations of spicy taste with temperature and with pain; (3) the tactile adjectives conceptualizing grasping-based sensations used for visual dimension (e.g., 烂 *lan4* 'tender'), and visual dimension adjectives utilized for tactile grasping-based sensations (e.g., 细 *xi4* 'thin'), both of which demonstrate the neural co-activation of touch and vision in perceiving shapes; and (4) visual color adjectives used for auditory pitch (e.g., 亮 *liang4* 'bright'). and auditory adjectives employed for visual brightness (e.g., 喧闹 *xuan1-nao4* 'noisy'), both of which suggest a neural connection between visual brightness and auditory pitch. Nevertheless, the biological association basis is not the only mechanism underlying linguistic synaesthesia in Mandarin sensory adjectives. Rather, biological association, perceived similarity, and sensory integration work collectively in Mandarin synaesthesia (see Chaps. 3 through 5).

To summarize, the fact that the patterns of Mandarin synaesthesia show language-specific characteristics when compared with the patterns of English synaesthesia does not support the cross-linguistic universality of synaesthetic tendencies proposed by the biological association account for linguistic synaesthesia. In addition, a biological association basis is only one of three underlying mechanisms for linguistic synaesthesia.

7.1.3 An Incorporated Theoretical Model

Zhao et al. (2018b) proposed that the distributions of Mandarin gustatory adjectives with synaesthetic uses could not be predicted by a single theory (i.e., either the embodiment account or the biological association account for linguistic synaesthesia), but could be explained by an incorporated approach containing both embodiment and biological mechanisms. As elaborated above, the synaesthetic usages of Mandarin sensory adjectives confirms this proposal as they suggest three kinds of mechanisms underlying linguistic synaesthesia. Specifically, perceived similarity and sensory integration are both embodiment mechanisms, which relate to bodily experiences or interactions with external human environments (Johnson 1987). In contrast, neural association is the biological mechanism shaped by the structure of human brains.

Thus, the incorporated model for linguistic synaesthesia can account for the general directional tendencies of Mandarin synaesthesia. Specifically, the embodiment mechanism underlying linguistic synaesthesia follows the general cognitive principle, mapping from more embodied to less embodied (Lakoff and Johnson 1980). It makes sense, then, that the synaesthetic transfers of Mandarin sensory adjectives would transfer from more embodied modalities to less embodied ones. However, motivation by a biological mechanism could result in synaesthetic mappings in both directions between two senses (Rakova 2003), resulting in synaesthetic transfers between modalities, such as grasping-based tactile perceptions and visual dimension mentioned above. Hence, an underlying biological mechanism makes synaesthetic transfers from less embodied to more embodied possible. Therefore, the tendency-based rather than absolute directionality of Mandarin synaesthesia would result from the interactions between the embodiment mechanism and the biological mechanism.

The incorporated model for linguistic synaesthesia can also explain language-specific characteristics of linguistic synaesthesia in Mandarin Chinese. Although the biological mechanism, based on the structure of human brains and therefore shared across the species, tends to result in analogous patterns of linguistic synaesthesia across different languages, the embodiment mechanism is based in bodily experiences that are subject to differences in surrounding environments. Thus, the bi-directional tendency of linguistic synaesthesia between touch and taste attested in Mandarin and not English would likely be caused by the dominance of taste in Chinese culture. For instance, Wang (1996) has found that food culture plays an important role in the creation and representation of Chinese characters. Xiong and Huang (2016) has demonstrated the synaesthetic versatility of the Chinese concept 味 *wei4* 'taste' in Buddhist texts, which can be used for the other four senses. Both studies indicate the great cultural impact of gustation in the linguistic behaviors of the Chinese language. While more systematic evidence is needed to completely establish that gustatory experiences exhibit a greater cultural dominance among speakers of Chinese than English, the hypothesis would provide a way to explain Mandarin-specific characteristics of synaesthetic transfers between touch and taste. That is, although touch, with its sensory receptors all over the body, is more embodied than taste, which has only sensory receptors in the mouth (Lehrer 1978; Shen 1997), the cultural dominance of gustation in Mandarin may reduce the differences of embodiment degrees between touch and taste. Thus, the preference of synaesthetic transfers from touch to taste is lowered in Mandarin Chinese.[1,2]

To summarize, the incorporated theoretical model of linguistic synaesthesia based in both embodiment and biological mechanisms not only accounts for the

[1]With respect to language-specific characteristics of Mandarin synaesthesia, it is notable that Mandarin compound adjectives have also been found with synaesthetic usages (see Chap. 6), while there has been no English compound adjective reported to be involved in linguistic synaesthesia (see appendices in Williams 1976: 475–476; Strik Lievers 2015: 92–93). Therefore, word formation would also be likely to provoke differences in the synaesthetic patterns of Mandarin and English.

[2]For the synaesthetic transfers found in Mandarin but not in Indo-European languages, such as the mappings from touch to smell and from taste to vision, the reason such examples were found in this study may lie in the fact that this study is based on a much larger data sample than those used for linguistic synesthesia in Indo-European languages. For instance, the data utilized in this study is four times as large as that used by Williams (1976) with respect to lexical types, and 16 times larger than the data utilized by Strik Lievers (2015) in terms of lexical tokens.

general tendencies of Mandarin synaesthesia (i.e., it being tendency-based rather than absolute in directionality), but also can predict language-specific characteristics of linguistic synaesthesia in Mandarin Chinese (i.e., the bi-directional transfer pattern between touch and taste). As the tendency-based directionality of linguistic synaesthesia has also been attested in Indo-European languages and non-Indo-European languages such as Hebrew (e.g., Shen 1997; Strik Lievers 2015), it is reasonable to assume that linguistic synaesthesia in these languages is also grounded in both embodiment and biological mechanisms, rather than one single mechanism exclusively. Thus, the incorporated theoretical model proposed for Mandarin synaesthesia would be applicable to linguistic synaesthesia across languages.

7.2 The Nature of Linguistic Synaesthesia Revisited

As elaborated in Sect. 1.1.3, linguistic synaesthesia has been called metaphorical (e.g., Strik Lievers 2017), neurological (e.g., Rakova 2003), or literal (e.g., Winter 2019b) by nature. The synaesthetic tendencies of Mandarin synaesthesia, however, do not support neither the neurological nor the literal view of linguistic synaesthesia.

Winter (2019b) suggested that linguistic and neurological synesthesia differed in their parameters, such as prevalence, types of mappings, specific mappings, sensation, and voluntary control, arguing against the neurological nature of linguistic synesthesia. The current study on Mandarin synaesthesia can offer further evidence to strengthen this position. Specifically, linguistic synesthesia was found to show prevalent distributions exhibiting systematic preferences for transfer directions (see Chaps. 2 through 7). Thus, linguistic synaesthesia is distinct from neurological synesthesia, which is uncommon with "the idiosyncratic nature" (Cytowic 2002 [1989]: 66). In addition, linguistic synaesthesia shows culturally-bounded, language-specific characteristics in Mandarin Chinese (see Sect. 7.1.2). Hence, linguistic synaesthesia is different from neurological synaesthesia, as neurological synaesthesia was found to demonstrate similar characteristics among people with distinct linguistic backgrounds (Asano and Yokosawa 2012; Hung et al. 2014). Furthermore, with respect to underlying mechanisms, Mandarin synesthesia is grounded in both embodiment and neural mechanisms, while neurological synesthesia was generally recognized to be motivated only by hard-wired neural mechanisms (Ramachandran and Hubbard 2001; Cytowic 2002 [1989]).

Winter's (2019b) assumption that linguistic synaesthesia is literal is also problematic. First, he did not give a definition of "literal". For instance, he considered the expression *sweet fragrance* to be the literal usage of *sweet*, as he treated taste and smell as integrated aspects of the same sense. One important piece of empirical evidence Winter relied on was the modality exclusivity data of different sensory words reported in Lynott and Connell (2009) and Lynott and Connell (2013). This data shows that most sensory words belong to multiple sensory modalities with varying degrees of exclusivity. However, Lynott and Connell (2009) and Lynott and Connell (2013) also demonstrated that most sensory words in English have dominant sensory domains. For instance, *sweet* received the highest score as a gustatory word in Lynott and Connell's (2009) rating task. That is, in terms of exclusivity, *sweet* is moderately exclusive for the gustatory sense over other sensory modalities (including smell). Thus, the data can be interpreted in different ways depending on whether the multi-modal aspect or the degree of exclusivity aspect is emphasized. Second, Winter (2019a, b) argued for the literal nature of linguistic synaesthesia based on the notion that a group of synesthetic words have an evaluative function which, by its nature, does not refer to the senses and hence should not be considered synesthetic. However, taking the evaluative valence into consideration does not refute the metaphorical uses of lexical items. For instance, one would argue a shift in the evaluative valence from a more concrete domain to a less concrete domain can also be observed in typical metaphorical expressions involving sensory items (e.g., *a bitter man*, 心里很苦 *xin1 li3 hen3 ku3* 'feel bitter in heart [sad, despondent]') (Lehrer 1978: 98; Zhao et al. 2018b: 1180). Last but not least, Winter's (2019a, b) literal claim could not account for the directional tendencies of linguistic synesthesia, which have been confirmed by the current study based on a comprehensive data sample for Mandarin sensory adjectives.

Section 1.1.3 establishes that linguistic synaesthesia does not share the same patterns with canonical metaphors. For instance, linguistic synaesthesia manifests itself as a mapping from one bodily domain to another bodily domain, while canonical metaphors generally map from bodily experiences to non-bodily experiences. In addition, linguistic synaesthesia has been attested to show a tendency-based directionality, while canonical metaphors have not been found to exhibit this pattern. Furthermore, linguistic synaesthesia is grounded not only in embodied cognition and biology itself, whereas canonical metaphors have been widely recognized to be motivated solely by the embodiment mechanism. This explains why linguistic synaesthesia has received little attention from the perspective of the theories of metaphors, particularly CMT, which is primarily related to metaphorical mappings from concrete to abstract with "implicit target domains" (Gibbs 2011: 530–531). Nevertheless, given the tendencies of Mandarin synaesthesia, one could observe that linguistic synaesthesia does show some similar characteristics as canonical metaphors.

First, canonical metaphors are employed systematically in both poetic and non-poetic languages, in accordance with CMT (Lakoff and Johnson 1980; Lakoff 1993; Gibbs 2011). Similarly, the widespread and systematic uses of linguistic synaesthesia in poetic and non-poetic languages have also been demonstrated by various studies. Ullmann (1966 [1963]) found that linguistic synaesthesia exists cross-linguistically, and Ullmann (1957), Shen (1997), and Yu (2003) reported poetic usages of linguistic synaesthesia in different languages (e.g., English, French, Hungary, Hebrew, and Mandarin). Williams (1976), Strik Lievers (2015), and Zhao et al. (2018b) established pervasive uses of linguistic synaesthesia in different non-poetic languages, such as English, Italian. In addition, the large data sample in this study (see Chap. 2) also suggests the abundant usages of linguistic synaesthesia.

Second, classic studies on conceptual metaphors, such as Lakoff and Johnson (1980) and Lakoff (1993), have proposed that metaphors tend to preserve the cognitive topology of source domains; namely, they follow the invariance principle. This study has confirmed the invariance hypothesis for linguistic synaesthesia in Mandarin sensory adjectives. For instance, Mandarin sensory adjectives generally preserve their polarities of perceptual intensity or affective evaluation when used in linguistic synaesthesia.

Third, Ahrens (2002) and Gibbs (2011) established the cognitive reality of metaphors in language comprehension. For example, metaphors following the general principle of mapping from the more accessible to the less accessible received higher acceptability and interpretability than metaphors violating this principle (Ahrens 2002). With respect to the cognitive reality of linguistic synaesthesia, experimental studies conducted by Shen and his colleagues (Shen 1997; Shen and Cohen 1998; Shen and Eisenman 2008; Shen and Gadir 2009), and Werning et al. (2006) have also demonstrated that the comprehension of synaesthetic expressions is also influenced by mapping directions from more embodied to less embodied, analogous to canonical metaphors. For example, Shen and his colleagues found that synaesthetic expressions following the mapping principle are easier to interpret and recall, and are judged as more natural than expressions violating the principle.

Last but not least, as suggested by El Refaie (2015) to interpret image metaphors as conceptual metaphors, linguistic synaesthesia can also fulfill a wide range of communicative and conceptual functions, similar to canonical metaphors. These communicative and conceptual functions include "attracting our attention, providing imaginative pleasure, and helping us to understand and evaluate particular conceptual domains" (El Refaie 2015: 74). Take the Mandarin synaesthetic expression 尖锐的笛音 *jian1-rui4 de di2-yin1* 'the sharp sound of the flute' for example. This expression would more easily evoke peoples' attention, compared to non-synaesthetic descriptions for the sound of the flute, such as 好听的笛音 *hao3-ting1 de di2-yin1* 'the melodious sound of the flute' or 难听的笛音 *nan2-ting1 de di2-yin1* 'the unpleasant sound of the flute'. In addition, the expression 尖锐的笛音 *jian1-rui4 de di2-yin1* 'the sharp sound of the flute' could also help people to understand the property of the sound through a conceptual relation to the sharp property of knives, so that people obtain a much more vivid grasp of the auditory domain. As the modifier 尖锐 *jian1-rui4* 'sharp' connotes a negative evaluation for touch in the source domain, which still implies an unpleasant feeling for the sound of the flute in the synaesthetic expression 尖锐的笛音 *jian1-rui4 de di2-yin1* 'the sharp sound of the flute', the evaluative function of linguistic synaesthesia is clear.

Linguistic synaesthesia mapping from a concrete source to a concrete target shares the same essential characteristics with canonical metaphors that map from the concrete to the abstract as linguistic realizations of conceptual metaphors. These shared characteristics include: (1) showing pervasive and systematic uses in both poetic and non-poetic languages, (2) following the invariance principle,

(3) exhibiting the cognitive reality of mapping directionality in language comprehension, and (4) fulfilling communicative and conceptual functions. Therefore, linguistic synaesthesia is metaphorical by nature and thus should be taken into consideration by CMT.

7.3 A Finer-Grained Account of Embodiment

In order to account for linguistic synaesthesia, CMT should be refined to incorporate the unique characteristics of this phenomenon.

The first distinctive characteristic of linguistic synaesthesia is its mapping from one bodily experience to another. CMT has proposed that human bodily experiences provide a cognitive basis for metaphors, and that experiences involving bodily contact and bodily interactions with surrounding environments are more embodied (Lakoff and Johnson 1980; Johnson 1987). Thus, concepts representing these experiences are more accessible, which are then generally employed to express less accessible concepts representing less embodied experiences (Lakoff and Johnson 1980; Johnson 1987). Although the theory is not confined to the dichotomy of bodily versus non-bodily experiences, linguistic studies following the theory mainly focus on the conceptualization of non-bodily experiences in terms of bodily experiences (e.g., Sweetser 1990; Lien 2005; among many others). However, linguistic synaesthesia could suggest that the dichotomy is insufficient for metaphors, as conceptual mappings from the embodied to the embodied also have realizations in the language. Furthermore, though both the source and target domains of linguistic synaesthesia are embodied, they exhibit different degrees of embodiment. For instance, touch and taste are the most embodied, vision follows, and hearing is less embodied, while smell is the least embodied in Mandarin Chinese (see Sect. 5.4). The degree of embodiment is a crucial concept currently lacking in CMT and required for a complete discussion of linguistic synaesthesia. In other words, experiences should be characterized in terms of a continuum from strongly embodied to strongly dis-embodied events, rather than according to a dichotomy between bodily and non-bodily events in the framework of CMT. It is interesting to note that Ahrens (2002) proposed that mapping principles, or underlying motivations in metaphorical mappings between source domains and target domains, are crucial for CMT to constrain and predict metaphorical mappings. The concept of degrees of embodiment proposed by this study could suggest that the specification of source domains in metaphorical mappings is also important for CMT to strengthen its theoretical powers of explanation and prediction.

The type of embodied events is another important notion to enrich CMT through the inclusion of patterns found in linguistic synaesthesia. Linguistic synaesthesia exhibits a tendency-based directionality that is grounded in both embodiment and biological mechanisms, and its tendency-based directionality results from interactions between those mechanisms. Therefore, it is important for the framework of CMT to include the biological mechanism as one of the embodied bases for metaphors. As pointed out by Rakova (2003), no consensus exists in what kinds of events can be regarded as embodied activities for cognitive representations. For instance, linguists generally recognize bodily interaction and coupling with the external environment as embodied activities (e.g., Lakoff and Johnson 1980; Johnson 1987). Cognitive scientists, however, consider neural activations in the brain as embodied activities (e.g., Winter 2016a; Meteryard et al. 2012). Linguistic synaesthesia grounded in both embodiment and biological mechanisms would suggest that both bodily interactions with external environments and neural activities in the brain are embodied events underlying linguistic representations, including metaphors. It is intriguing to note that increasingly studies such as Teng (2006: 83), Cacciari (2008), and Lakoff (2008) have suggested that neural activities "embedded in and appropriately coupled to" bodily interactions with surrounding environments underlie and constrain metaphorical conceptualizations in language.

CMT should consider the degree of embodiment and the type of embodied events to explain the unique characteristics of linguistic synaesthesia. The refined version of CMT would also be useful to examine other physiologically-based metaphorical representations. Take the image metaphor "*the folding bed is a crocodile*" identified by El Refaie (2015: 71) for example. Both the folding bed and the crocodile are concrete objects that can be experienced by human bodies. However, the crocodile as an animate object would be more accessible than the folding bed as an inanimate object, as the former can move, make sounds, and so forth, which could provide people with multiple embodied experiences. By adopting the refined version of CMT based on a finer-grained account of embodiment, the source and target domains of image metaphorical expression could be differentiated in terms of their degrees of embodiment, which would further explain the metaphorical mapping for the expression "*the folding bed is a crocodile*".

With respect to the finer-grained account of embodiment, it would facilitate the understanding of other cognitive behaviors apart from linguistic conceptualizations. Cognitive activities such as memory, reasoning, imagination, and so forth have also been widely recognized as grounded in embodiment (e.g., Gibbs 2005; Grady 2005; Meteryard et al. 2012; Pexman 2017). One implication of the finer-grained theory of embodiment for cognitive research, therefore, is that more attention should be paid to touch and taste rather than overwhelmingly to vision, as suggested by Popova (2005). That is because touch and taste exhibit higher degrees of embodiment than vision evidenced by linguistic synaesthesia.

7.4 Summary of Theoretical Implications

This chapter has examined the theoretical implications of linguistic synaesthesia for the wider field. Both the embodiment account and the biological association account for linguistic synaesthesia are insufficient to explain and predict the tendencies found in Mandarin synaesthesia. Thus, an incorporated theoretical model containing both embodiment and biological mechanisms has been suggested. In addition, as linguistic synaesthesia can be considered a kind of metaphor that is a linguistic realization of conceptual metaphors, analogous to canonical metaphors that map from the concrete to the abstract, linguistic synaesthesia is metaphorical by nature as an embodied conceptualization. In order to explain linguistic synaesthesia under the framework of CMT, I argued for a finer-grained account of embodiment to enrich the theory, where the notions of the degree of embodiment and the type of embodied events should be introduced.

There is another interesting implication of linguistic synaesthesia from a non-linguistic perspective that should be mentioned. Although linguistic synaesthesia is not neurological by nature (see Sect. 7.2), linguistic synaesthesia shows some similarities with neurological synaesthesia. For instance, Ronga et al.'s (2012) corpus-based study showed that the associations between touch and hearing and between vision and hearing demonstrated similar tendencies in linguistic synesthesia and neurological synesthesia. Analogously, this study identified frequent associations between color and sound (see Chap. 5) in Mandarin synaesthesia, which also exist in neurological synaesthesia (e.g., Marks 1978; Day 1996; Ward et al. 2006). Furthermore, an underlying neural mechanism may also be shared by both types of synesthesia. Thus, the fact that linguistic synaesthesia is grounded in multiple mechanisms would imply that neurological synaesthesia may not be motivated by the neural mechanism exclusively. It is intriguing to note that linguistic concepts can also induce neurological synaesthesia, such as lexical-gustatory synaesthesia (Banissy et al. 2014), which might indicate that the conceptual system also plays a role in underlying neurological synaesthesia. Given the focus on linguistic synaesthesia in this book, I cannot further explore this here. Nevertheless, the connections between linguistic synesthesia and neurological synesthesia represent a fascinating but challenging issue in the scientific field, and our understanding of the brain and human cognition would be greatly enhanced through its further exploration.

References

Ahrens, Kathleen. 2002. When love is not digested: Underlying reasons for source to target domain pairings in the contemporary theory of metaphor. In *Proceedings of the first cognitive linguistics conference*, 273–302.

Amedi, Amir, Gilad Jacobson, Talma Hendler, Rafael Malach, and Ehud Zohary. 2002. Convergence of visual and tactile shape processing in the human lateral occipital complex. *Cerebral Cortex* 12 (11): 1202–1212.

Asano, Michiko, and Kazuhiko Yokosawa. 2012. Synesthetic colors for Japanese late acquired graphemes. *Consciousness and Cognition* 21: 983–993.

Banissy, Michael, Clare Jonas, and Roi Cohen Kadosh. 2014. Synesthesia: An introduction. *Frontiers in Psychology* 5 (1414): 1–3.

Cacciari, Cristina. 2008. Crossing the senses in metaphorical language. In *The Cambridge handbook of metaphor and thought*, ed. Raymond Gibbs, 425–443. New York: Cambridge University Press.

Cytowic, Richard. 2002 [1989]. *Synesthesia: A union of the senses*, 2nd ed. Cambridge: The MIT Press.

Day, Sean. 1996. Synaesthesia and synaesthetic metaphors. *Psyche* 2 (32): 1–16.

Elisabeth, El Refaie. 2015. Reconsidering "image metaphor" in the light of perceptual simulation theory. *Metaphor and Symbol* 30 (1): 63–76.

Gibbs, Raymond W. 2005. *Embodiment and cognitive science*. New York: Cambridge University Press.

Gibbs, Raymond W. 2011. Evaluating conceptual metaphor theory. *Discourse Processes* 48 (8): 529–562.

Grady, Joseph. 2005. Primary metaphors as inputs to conceptual integration. *Journal of Pragmatics* 37 (10): 1595–1614.

Hung, Wan-Yu., Julia Simner, Richard Shillcock, and David M. Eagleman. 2014. Synesthesia in Chinese characters: The role of radical function and position. *Consciousness and Cognition* 24: 38–48.

Johnson, Mark. 1987. *The body in the mind: The bodily basis of meaning, imagination, and reason*. Chicago: University of Chicago Press.

Lakoff, George. 1993. The contemporary theory of metaphor. In *Metaphor and thought*, 2nd ed, ed. Andrew Ortony, 202–251. New York and Melbourne: Cambridge University Press.

Lakoff, George. 2008. The neural theory of metaphor. In *The Cambridge handbook of metaphor and thought*, ed. Raymond W. Gibbs, 17–38. New York: Cambridge University Press.

Lakoff, George, and Mark Johnson. 1980. *Metaphors we live by*. Chicago: University of Chicago Press.

Lehrer, Adrienne. 1978. Structures of the lexicon and transfer of meaning. *Lingua* 45 (2): 95–123.

Lien, Chinfa. 2005. Verbs of visual perception in Taiwanese Southern Min: A cognitive approach to shift of semantic domains. *Language and Linguistics* 6 (1): 109–132.

Lynott, Dermot, and Louise Connell. 2009. Modality exclusivity norms for 423 object properties. *Behavior research methods* 41 (2): 558–564.

Lynott, Dermot, and Louise Connell. 2013. Modality exclusivity norms for 400 nouns: The relationship between perceptual experience and surface word form. *Behavior research methods* 45 (2): 516–526.

Marks, Lawrence E. 1978. *The unity of the senses: Interrelations among the modalities*. New York: Academic Press.

Meteyard, Lotte, Sara Rodriguez Cuadrado, Bahador Bahrami, and Gabriella Vigliocco. 2012. Coming of age: A review of embodiment and the neuroscience of semantics. *Cortex* 48 (7): 788–804.

Miller, George, and Philip Johnson-Laird. 1976. *Language and perception*. Cambridge, London and Melbourne: Cambridge University Press.

Pexman, Penny M. 2017. The role of embodiment in conceptual development. *Language, Cognition and Neuroscience* 1–10.

Popova, Yanna. 2005. Image schemas and verbal synaesthesia. In *From perception to meaning: Image schema in cognitive linguistics (cognitive linguistics research 29)*, ed. Beate Hampe and Joseph Grady, 395–420. Berlin and New York: Mouton de Gruyter.

Purves, Dale, George J. Augustine, David Fitzpatrick, Lawrence C. Katz, Anthony-Samuel LaMantia, James O. McNamara, and S. Mark Williams (eds.). 2001 [2000]. *Neuroscience*, 2nd ed. Massachusetts: Sinauer Associates Inc.

Rakova, Marina. 2003. *The extent of the literal: Metaphor, polysemy and the theories of concepts*. Hampshire: Palgrave Macmillan.

Ramachandran, Vilayanur, and Edward Hubbard. 2001. Synaesthesia—A window into perception, thought and language. *Journal of Consciousness Studies* 8 (12): 3–34.

Ronga, Irene, Carla Bazzanella, Ferdinando Rossi, and Giandomenico Iannetti. 2012. Linguistic synaesthesia, perceptual synaesthesia, and the interaction between multiple sensory modalities. *Pragmatics & Cognition* 20 (1): 135–167.

Shen, Yeshayahu. 1997. Cognitive constraints on poetic figures. *Cognitive Linguistics* 8 (1): 33–71.

Shen, Yeshayahu, and Michal Cohen. 1998. How come silence is sweet but sweetness is not silent: A cognitive account of directionality in poetic synaesthesia. *Language and Literature* 7 (2): 123–140.

Shen, Yeshayahu, and David Eisenman. 2008. "Heard melodies are sweet, but those unheard are sweeter": Synaesthesia and cognition. *Language and Literature* 17 (2): 101–121.

Shen, Yeshayahu, and Osnat Gadir. 2009. How to interpret the music of caressing: Target and source assignment in synaesthetic genitive constructions. *Journal of Pragmatics* 41 (2): 357–371.

Strik Lievers, Francesca. 2015. Synaesthesia: A corpus-based study of cross-modal directionality. *Functions of Language* 22 (1): 69–95.

Strik Lievers, Francesca. 2017. Figures and the senses: Towards a definition of synaesthesia. *Review of Cognitive Linguistics* 15 (1): 83–101.

Sweetser, Eve. 1990. *From etymology to pragmatics: Metaphorical and cultural aspects of semantic structure*. Cambridge and New York: Cambridge University Press.

Teng, Norman Y. 2006. Metaphor and coupling: An embodied, action-oriented perspective. *Metaphor and Symbol* 21 (2): 67–85.

Ullmann, Stephen. 1957. *The principles of semantics*. Oxford: Basil Blackwell.

Ullmann, Stephen. 1966 [1963] Semantic universals. In *Universals of language*, 2nd ed, ed. J. Greenberg, 217–262. Cambridge and London: The MIT Press.

Wang, Ning (王宁). 1996. *The principle in etymological studies on Chinese* [训诂学原理]. Beijing [北京]: China International Radio Press [中国国际广播出版社].

Ward, Jamie, Brett Huckstep, and Elias Tsakanikos. 2006. Sound-colour synaesthesia: To what extent does it use cross-modal mechanisms common to us all? *Cortex* 42 (2): 264–280.

Werning, Markus, Jens Fleischhauer and Hakan Beseoglu. 2006. The cognitive accessibility of synaesthetic metaphors. In *Proceedings of the 28th annual conference of the cognitive science society*, 2365–2370.

Williams, Joseph. 1976. Synaesthetic adjectives: A possible law of sematic change. *Language* 52 (2): 461–478.

Winter, Bodo. 2016a. *The sensory structure of the English lexicon*. Merced dissertation, Merced, CA: University of California.

Winter, Bodo. 2019a. *Sensory linguistics: Language, perception and metaphor*. Amsterdam and Philadelphia: John Benjamins Publishing Company.

Winter, Bodo. 2019b. Synaesthetic metaphors are neither synaesthetic nor metaphorical. In *Perception metaphors*, ed. Laura J. Speed, Carolyn O'Meara, Lila San San, and Asifa Majid, 105–126. Amsterdam and Philadelphia: John Benjamins Publishing Company.

Xiong, Jiajuan and Chu-Ren Huang. 2016. The synaesthetic and metaphorical uses of 味 *wei4* 'taste'. In *Proceedings of the 30th Pacific Asia conference on language, information and computation (PACLIC-30)*, 485–492.

Yu, Ning. 2003. Synesthetic metaphors: A cognitive perspective. *Journal of Literary Semantics* 32 (1): 19–34.

Zhao, Qingqing (赵青青) and Chu-Ren Huang (黄居仁). 2018. Mapping models and underlying mechanisms of synaesthetic metaphors in Mandarin [现代汉语通感隐喻的映射模型与制约机制]. *Language Teaching and Linguistic Studies* [语言教学与研究] 1: 44–55.

Zhao, Qingqing, Chu-Ren Huang, and Yunfei Long. 2018b. Synaesthesia in Chinese: A corpus-based study on gustatory adjectives in Mandarin. *Linguistics* 56 (5): 1167–1194.

Chapter 8
Conclusion

This book has examined the tendencies of Mandarin synaesthesia and the theoretical implications of linguistic synaesthesia from a corpus-driven approach. With respect to the data collection for Mandarin synaesthesia, this study proposed a linguistic synaesthesia identification procedure (LSIP), which has been demonstrated to be applicable to identification of linguistic synaesthesia of other languages in other corpora. In addition, based on the distribution of synaesthetic uses of Mandarin sensory adjectives in the Sinica corpus, this study has found that: (1) Mandarin synaesthesia exhibits directionality mapping from more embodied modalities to less embodied ones, as predicted by the embodiment account of linguistic synaesthesia; (2) the directional patterns of Mandarin synaesthesia are tendencies-based rather than absolute, as the synaesthetic transfers violating the directionality have also been attested in Mandarin; (3) the tendencies of Mandarin synaesthesia show both commonality and specificity when compared to the attested patterns of English synaesthesia, which hence does not support the cross-lingual universality of synaesthetic tendencies suggested by the biological association account of linguistic synaesthesia; and (4) in terms of the mechanisms underlying linguistic synaesthesia, synaesthetic usages of Mandarin sensory adjectives not only suggest the perceived similarity basis of intensity and subjective evaluations, but also indicate the sensory integration basis and the neural connection basis for linguistic synaesthesia.

This study has also proposed an incorporated theoretical model containing both embodiment mechanisms and biological mechanisms to account for linguistic synaesthesia, as neither the embodiment account nor the biological association account of linguistic synaesthesia could fully predict the synaesthetic patterns of Mandarin sensory adjectives. Instead, the incorporated model not only could explain the tendencies of Mandarin synaesthesia, but also would predict the language-specific characteristics of linguistic synaesthesia in Mandarin Chinese. Furthermore, it has also been demonstrated that the incorporated theoretical model could explain synaesthetic patterns of other languages.

The important theoretical implications of linguistic synaesthesia for Conceptual Metaphor Theory and the embodiment theory have also been figured out. The study

Q. Zhao, *Embodied Conceptualization or Neural Realization*,
Frontiers in Chinese Linguistics 10, https://doi.org/10.1007/978-981-32-9315-1_8

has established that linguistic synaesthesia is also a kind of metaphor as a linguistic realization of conceptual metaphors, based on its pervasive usages in both poetic and ordinary languages, conformity to the invariance principle, cognitive reality in language comprehension, and communicative and conceptual functions. Therefore, Conceptual Metaphor Theory and the embodiment theory have been suggested to be refined, to explain the characteristics of linguistic synaesthesia. The book thus argued that the theories should include a finer-grained account of embodiment covering the notions of the degree of embodiment and the type of embodied events.

A corpus-driven approach such as the one employed in the current study would be ill-suited to study how neuro-cognitive mechanisms function exactly to underlie linguistic synaesthesia. However, if linguistic synaesthesia (and metaphors) does involve linguistic conceptualizations based on neuro-cognitive motivations, then corpus-driven distributions would offer direct evidence for how the bridge between neuro-cognitive activities and linguistic conventions of conceptualization could be built, and how such conventions would be formed differently for different languages. One of the future studies for the current research is to compare the attested patterns of Mandarin synaesthesia from the corpus-driven approach with those found by experimental methods, such as Chen et al.'s (2019) work on the exclusivity and competition of sensory modalities in Mandarin sensory words, for deeper and further understanding of linguistic synaesthesia (and metaphors) and eventually the nature of conceptualization and representation of meanings in human brains.

Reference

Chen, I-Hsuan, Qingqing Zhao, Yunfei Long, Qin Lu and Chu-Ren Huang. 2019. Mandarin Chinese modality exclusivity norms. PLoS ONE 14 (2): e0211336.

Appendix A
Distributions of Synaesthetic Uses of Mandarin Tactile Adjectives in the Sinica Corpus

Source domain	Target domain						Total
Touch	Taste	Smell	Vision			Hearing	
			Color	Dimension	Visual situation		
Intensity							
强 *qiang2* 'strong'	0	0	55	0	8	13	76
强烈 *qiang2-lie4* 'strong'	3	6	33	0	21	3	66
弱 *ruo4* 'weak'	0	0	12	0	8	16	36
Temperature							
冷 *leng3* 'cold'	0	1	14	0	35	117	167
热烈 *re4-lie4* 'scorching'	0	0	0	0	30	64	94
烈 *lie4* 'scorching'	78	0	0	0	13	0	91
热 *re4* 'hot'	0	1	1	0	46	0	48
寒 *han2* 'chilling'	0	0	22	0	9	2	33
温暖 *wen1-nuan3* 'warm'	0	2	9	0	11	3	25
冰冷 *bing1-leng3* 'ice-cold'	0	0	1	0	11	11	23
暖 *nuan3* 'warm'	0	0	22	0	0	0	22
灼灼 *zhuo2-zhuo2* 'scorching'	0	0	4	0	4	0	8
冷冰冰 *leng3-bing1-bing1* 'icy'	0	0	0	0	3	3	6
温 *wen1* 'lukewarm'	0	0	0	0	2	3	5
炽烈 *chi4-lie4* 'scorching'	0	0	3	0	2	0	5
炽热 *chi4-re4* 'scorching'	0	1	0	0	3	0	4
凛凛 *lin3-lin3* 'cold'	0	0	0	0	3	0	3
寒冷 *han2-leng3* 'cold'	0	0	0	0	1	1	2
冷冽 *leng3-lie4* 'piercingly cold'	0	0	0	0	2	0	2
火热 *huo3-re4* 'hot'	0	0	0	0	2	0	2
冰凉 *bing1-liang2* 'ice-cold'	0	0	0	0	0	1	1

(continued)

Q. Zhao, *Embodied Conceptualization or Neural Realization*,
Frontiers in Chinese Linguistics 10, https://doi.org/10.1007/978-981-32-9315-1

(continued)

Source domain	Target domain						Total
Touch	Taste	Smell	Vision			Hearing	
			Color	Dimension	Visual situation		
凉 *liang2* 'cool'	0	0	1	0	0	0	1
刺冽 *ci4-lie4* 'chilling'	0	0	1	0	0	0	1
干冷 *gan1-leng3* 'dry-cold'	0	0	0	0	1	0	1
Hardness							
烂 *lan4* 'tender'	0	0	0	109	8	0	117
温柔 *wen1-rou2* 'soft'	0	0	0	0	42	41	83
柔 *rou2* 'soft'	0	0	11	0	8	31	50
轻柔 *qing1-rou2* 'soft'	0	1	1	0	9	23	34
软 *ruan3* 'soft'	0	2	0	0	21	4	27
柔软 *rou2-ruan3* 'soft'	0	1	2	0	13	6	22
硬 *ying4* 'hard'	0	0	0	0	17	0	17
僵硬 *jiang1-ying4* 'stiff'	0	0	0	0	14	2	16
酥 *su1* 'crisp'	0	0	0	0	8	0	8
脆 *cui4* 'crisp'	0	0	0	0	0	7	7
轻脆 *qing1-cui4* 'crisp'	0	0	0	0	0	6	6
僵 *jiang1* 'stiff'	0	0	0	0	6	0	6
硬梆梆 *ying4-bang1-bang1* 'hard'	0	0	0	0	2	0	2
柔韧 *rou2-ren4* 'pliable'	0	0	0	0	0	1	1
坚硬 *jian1-ying* 'hard'	0	0	0	0	0	1	1
脆弱 *cui4-ruo4* 'fragile'	0	0	0	0	1	0	1
Sharpness							
尖 *jian1* 'sharp'	0	0	0	122	0	117	239
尖锐 *jian1-rui4* 'sharp'	0	0	0	10	2	21	33
锐利 *rui4-li4* 'sharp'	0	0	0	2	17	0	19
凌厉 *ling2-li4* 'sharp'	0	0	0	0	12	0	12
钝 *dun4* 'blunt'	0	0	1	4	1	3	9
犀利 *xi1-li4* 'sharp'	0	0	1	0	2	1	4
锐 *rui4* 'sharp'	0	0	0	0	0	2	2
尖利 *jian1-li4* 'sharp'	0	0	0	0	0	1	1
锋利 *feng1-li4* 'sharp'	0	0	0	0	1	0	1
Dampness							
干 *gan1* 'dry'	0	0	3	0	456	9	468
湿 *shi1* 'damp'	0	1	3	0	66	0	70
温润 *wen1-run4* 'moist'	0	1	6	0	3	1	11
湿润 *shi1-run4* 'moist'	0	0	0	0	8	0	8
干燥 *gan1-zao4* 'dry'	0	1	0	0	2	0	3
柔润 *rou2-run4* 'soft-moist'	0	0	0	0	0	1	1
濡湿 *ru4-shi1* 'damp'	0	0	0	0	1	0	1

(continued)

(continued)

Source domain	Target domain						Total
Touch	Taste	Smell	Vision			Hearing	
			Color	Dimension	Visual situation		
Smoothness							
粗 *cu1* 'rough'	0	0	0	133	0	7	140
涩 *se4* 'rough'	22	2	0	0	0	1	25
粗糙 *cu1-cao1* 'rough'	0	0	0	0	17	2	19
黏 *nian2* 'sticky'	0	0	0	0	8	3	11
滑 *hua2* 'smooth'	0	1	0	0	2	0	3
干涩 *gan1-se4* 'dry-rough'	0	0	0	0	0	2	2
滑溜溜 *hua2-liu1-liu1* 'smooth'	0	0	0	0	2	0	2
Physical force							
轻 *qing1* 'light (in weight)'	2	2	2	0	103	244	353
重 *zhong4* 'heavy'	17	7	3	0	18	40	85
笨重 *ben4-zhong4* 'heavy'	0	0	0	0	10	1	11
强劲 *qiang2-jing4* 'of strong force'	1	0	0	0	7	0	8
笨 *ben4* 'heavy'	0	0	0	0	3	0	3
粗重 *cu1-zhong4* 'heavy'	0	0	0	0	1	1	2
Pain							
胀 *zhang4* 'swelling (in pain)'	0	0	0	22	0	0	22
软弱 *ruan3-ruo4* 'feeble'	0	0	0	0	2	2	4
麻 *ma2* 'trembling'	2	0	0	0	0	0	2
刺 *ci4* 'stabbing'	0	0	0	0	1	0	1
Total	125	30	211	402	1109	818	2695

Appendix B
Distributions of Synaesthetic Uses of Mandarin Gustatory Adjectives in the Sinica Corpus

Source domain	Target domain						Total
Taste	Touch	Smell	Vision			Hearing	
			Color	Dimension	Visual situation		
Intensity							
淡 *dan4* 'of mild taste'	0	27	212	0	38	71	348
浓 *nong2* 'of intense taste'	0	33	34	0	133	5	205
Quality							
美 *mei3* 'tasty'	0	1	0	0	1222	23	1246
酸 *suan1* 'sour'	90	10	0	0	0	1	101
鲜 *xian1* 'tasty'	0	0	83	0	0	0	83
辣 *la4* 'hot (in taste)'	2	0	0	0	78	0	80
苦 *ku3* 'bitter'	1	1	0	0	66	1	69
甜美 *tian2-mei3* 'tasty'	0	1	1	0	29	26	57
甜 *tian2* 'sweet'	0	13	2	0	13	8	36
甜蜜 *tian2-mi4* 'sweet'	0	3	0	0	10	3	16
油腻 *you2-ni4* 'greasy'	5	2	0	0	5	0	12
腻 *ni4* 'greasy'	6	0	0	0	3	1	10
辛辣 *xin1-la4* 'hot (in taste)'	0	7	0	0	0	0	7
甜腻 *tian2-ni4* 'overly sweet'	0	4	0	0	0	2	6
咸 *xian2* 'salty'	0	5	0	0	0	0	5
辛 *xin1* 'hot (in taste)'	0	3	0	0	0	0	3
鲜美 *xian1-mei3* 'tasty'	0	0	1	0	1	0	2
甘 *gan1* 'sweet'	0	2	0	0	0	0	2
甘甜 *gan1-tian2* 'sweet'	0	1	0	0	0	0	1
甘美 *gan1-mei3* 'tasty'	0	0	0	0	0	1	1
甘醇 *gan1-chu2* 'luscious'	0	1	0	0	0	0	1
Total	104	114	333	0	1598	142	2291

Q. Zhao, *Embodied Conceptualization or Neural Realization*,
Frontiers in Chinese Linguistics 10, https://doi.org/10.1007/978-981-32-9315-1

Appendix C
Distributions of Synaesthetic Uses of Mandarin Visual Adjectives in the Sinica Corpus

Source domain	Target domain				Total
Vision	Touch	Taste	Smell	Hearing	
Color					
清 *qing1* 'limpid'	21	26	38	31	116
清楚 *qing1-chu3* 'clear'	0	0	1	62	63
杂 *za2* 'varicolored'	0	1	6	53	60
清晰 *qing1-xi1* 'clear'	0	0	0	34	34
清爽 *qing1-shuang3* 'clear'	13	12	3	0	28
幽幽 *you1-you1* 'faint'	0	0	1	18	19
爽朗 *shuang3-lang3* 'clear'	1	0	0	12	13
隐隐 *yin3-yin3* 'faint'	2	0	2	7	11
明亮 *ming2-liang4* 'bright'	0	0	0	7	7
清亮 *qing1-liang4* 'bright'	0	0	0	6	6
暗 *an4* 'dark'	0	0	3	3	6
透明 *tou4-ming2* 'transparent'	0	0	0	4	4
朗朗 *lang3-lang3* 'bright'	0	0	0	3	3
明朗 *ming2-lang3* 'bright'	0	0	0	3	3
清纯 *qing1-chun2* 'clear'	0	0	0	3	3
混浊 *hun2-zhuo2* 'turbid'	0	0	0	3	3
清澈 *qing1-che4* 'limpid'	0	0	0	3	3
亮 *liang4* 'bright'	0	0	0	2	2
纯净 *chun2-jing4* 'pure'	0	0	0	2	2
清白 *qing1-bai2* 'clear white'	0	1	0	0	1
黯然 *an4-ran2* 'dark'	0	0	0	1	1
开朗 *kai1-lang3* 'clear'	0	0	0	1	1
明晰 *ming2-xi1* 'clear'	0	0	0	1	1
清朗 *qing1-lang3* 'clear and bright'	0	0	0	1	1

(continued)

Q. Zhao, *Embodied Conceptualization or Neural Realization*, Frontiers in Chinese Linguistics 10, https://doi.org/10.1007/978-981-32-9315-1

(continued)

Source domain	Target domain				Total
Vision	Touch	Taste	Smell	Hearing	
澄澈 *cheng2-che4* 'clear'	0	0	0	1	1
澄净 *cheng2-jing4* 'clean and clear'	0	0	0	1	1
浑 *hun2* 'turbid	0	0	0	1	1
浑沌 *hun2-dun4* 'turbid'	0	0	0	1	1
清澄 *qing1-cheng2* 'limpid'	0	0	0	1	1
氤氲 *yin1-yun4* 'enshrouding'	0	0	1	0	1
Dimension					
大 *da4* 'big'	0	0	1	1083	1084
高 *gao1* 'high'	0	0	0	197	197
低 *di1* 'low'	0	0	0	182	182
小 *xiao3* 'small'	0	0	0	84	84
长 *chang2* 'long'	0	0	0	77	77
沉 *chen2* 'deep'	6	0	1	67	74
低沉 *di1-chen2* 'low'	0	0	0	45	45
细 *xi4* 'thin'	8	0	0	27	35
高亢 *gao1-kang4* 'high'	0	0	0	26	26
巨大 *ju4-da4* 'huge'	0	0	0	16	16
深 *shen1* 'deep'	0	0	0	16	16
肥 *fei2* 'fat'	0	14	0	0	14
薄 *bao2* 'thin'	1	3	1	1	6
浅 *qian3* 'shallow'	0	1	0	5	6
浑厚 *hun2-hou4* 'very thick'	0	1	0	5	6
深沉 *shen1-chen2* 'deep'	0	0	0	6	6
厚 *hou4* 'thick'	0	4	0	1	5
短 *duan3* 'short'	0	0	0	3	3
细微 *xi4-wei1* 'thin'	0	0	0	3	3
纤细 *xian1-xi4* 'very thin'	0	0	0	3	3
扁 *bian3* 'flat'	0	0	0	2	2
短促 d*uan3-cu4* 'very short'	0	0	0	2	2
绵长 *mian2-chang2* 'very long'	0	0	0	2	2
细碎 *xi4-sui4* 'fragmented'	0	0	0	2	2
丰厚 *feng1-hou4* 'thick'	0	0	0	1	1
浩大 *hao4-da4* 'huge'	0	0	0	1	1
宏大 *hong2-da4* 'huge'	0	0	0	1	1
宽广 *kuang1-guang3* 'broad'	0	0	0	1	1
宽厚 *kuan1-hou4* 'broad and thick'	0	0	0	1	1
深厚 *shen1-hou4* 'deep and thick'	0	1	0	0	1
微小 *wei1-xiao3* 'very small'	0	0	0	1	1

(continued)

(continued)

Source domain	Target domain				Total
Vision	Touch	Taste	Smell	Hearing	
细小 *xi4-xiao3* 'thin and small'	0	0	0	1	1
阴沉 *yin1-chen2* 'of low sky'	0	0	0	1	1
Visual situation					
紧 *jin3* 'tense (in vision)'	409	0	0	2	411
松 *song1* 'shaggy'	116	0	0	0	116
嫩 *nen4* 'delicate'	45	0	0	1	46
幽静 *you1-jing1* 'graceful'	0	0	0	25	25
松弛 *song-chi2* 'slack'	14	0	0	0	14
沉静 *chen2-jing4* 'still'	0	0	0	12	12
紧绷 *jin3-beng1* 'taut (in vision)'	11	0	0	0	11
细致 *xi4-zhi4* 'exquisite'	4	0	1	5	10
细嫩 *xi4-nen4* 'delicate'	7	0	0	2	9
清静 *qing1-jing4* 'secluded'	0	0	0	8	8
激昂 *ji1-ang2* 'aroused'	0	0	0	7	7
绵绵 *mian2-mian2* 'continuous'	6	0	0	1	7
娇滴滴 *jiao1-di1-di1* 'delicately pretty'	0	0	0	5	5
紧密 *jin3-mi4* 'close'	5	0	0	0	5
稚嫩 *zhi4-nen4* 'young (in vision)'	0	0	0	5	5
昂扬 *ang2-yang2* 'soared'	0	0	0	4	4
紧迫 *jin3-po4* 'close'	0	0	0	4	4
清幽 *qing1-you1* 'graceful'	0	0	4	0	4
空白 *kong1-bai2* 'blank'	0	0	0	3	3
苍老 *cang1-lao3* 'aged'	0	0	0	3	3
毛茸茸 *mao2-rong2-rong2* 'hairy'	3	0	0	0	3
密集 *mi4-ji2* 'dense'	0	0	0	3	3
稀落 *xi1-luo4* 'sparse'	0	0	0	3	3
亮丽 *liang4-li4* 'beautiful'	0	0	0	2	2
缠绵 *chan2-mian2* 'continuous'	0	0	0	1	1
稠 *chou2* 'dense'	0	0	0	1	1
大方 *da4-fang1* 'graceful'	0	0	0	1	1
滚滚 *gun3-gun3* 'billowing'	0	0	0	1	1
娇媚 *jiao4-mei4* 'charming'	0	0	0	1	1
紧凑 *jin3-cou4* 'compact'	0	0	0	1	1
连绵 *lian2-mian2* 'continuous'	0	0	0	1	1
绵密 *mian2-mi4* 'dense'	0	0	0	1	1
清丽 *qing1-li4* 'elegantly beautiful'	0	0	0	1	1
清逸 *qing1-yi4* 'elegant'	0	0	0	1	1
松垮 *song1-kua3* 'baggy'	1	0	0	0	1
致密 *zhi4-mi4* 'dense'	0	0	0	1	1
Total	673	64	63	2234	3034

Appendix D
Distributions of Synaesthetic Uses of Mandarin Auditory Adjectives in the Sinica Corpus

Source domain	Target domain						Total
Hearing	Touch	Taste	Smell	Vision			
				Color	Dimension	Visual situation	
和谐 *he2-xie2* 'harmonious'	0	0	0	3	0	23	26
喧闹 *xuan1-nao4* 'noisy'	0	0	0	2	0	0	2
吵 *chao3* 'loud'	0	0	0	1	0	0	1
喧哗 *xuan1-hua2* 'noisy'	0	0	0	1	0	0	1
Total	0	0	0	7	0	23	30

Q. Zhao, *Embodied Conceptualization or Neural Realization*,
Frontiers in Chinese Linguistics 10, https://doi.org/10.1007/978-981-32-9315-1

Appendix E
Distributions of Synaesthetic Uses of Mandarin Olfactory Adjectives in the Sinica Corpus

Source domain	Target domain						Total
SMELL	Touch	Taste	Vision			Hearing	
			Color	Dimension	Visual situation		
香 *xiang1* 'fragrant'	0	22	0	0	0	0	22
臭 *chou4* 'smelly'	0	0	0	0	10	0	10
Total	0	22	0	0	10	0	32

Q. Zhao, *Embodied Conceptualization or Neural Realization*,
Frontiers in Chinese Linguistics 10, https://doi.org/10.1007/978-981-32-9315-1

Bibliography

The Dictionary Office in the Institute of Linguistics from Chinese Academy of Social Sciences (中国社会科学院语言研究所词典编辑室). 2012. *Contemporary Chinese Dictionary* [现代汉语词典] (6th ed.). Beijing [北京]: The Commercial Press [商务印书馆].

Werning, M., J. Fleischhauer and H. Beseoglu. The cognitive accessibility of synaesthetic metaphors. In *Proceedings of the 28th annual conference of the cognitive science society* 2006 (pp. 2365–2370).

Q. Zhao, *Embodied Conceptualization or Neural Realization*,
Frontiers in Chinese Linguistics 10, https://doi.org/10.1007/978-981-32-9315-1

The manufacturer's authorised representative in the EU is Springer Nature Customer Service Centre GmbH, Europaplatz 3, 69115 Heidelberg, Germany. If you have any concerns regarding our products, please contact ProductSafety@springernature.com

Printed and bound by CPI Group (UK) Ltd, Croydon, CR0 4YY
25/09/2026
02222898-0019